LAND OF THE FREE

A Journey to the American Dream

LAND OF THE FREE

A Journey to the American Dream

GENERAL EDITOR:
DAVID SEAN PALUDEINE

INTRODUCTION BY BILL YENNE

GRAMERCY BOOKS
NEW YORK

First published in 1998 by
PRC Publishing Ltd,
Kiln House, 210 New Kings Road, London SW6 4NZ

This edition was produced by American Graphic Systems, Inc.
Design and text © 1998 American Graphic Systems, Inc.
Designed and captioned by Bill Yenne, with design assistance by Azia Yenne.
Proofreading by Amy Bokser and Joan B. Hayes.

This edition is published by Gramercy Books,®
a division of Random House Value Publishing, Inc.,
201 East 50th Street, New York, New York, 10022.

Gramercy Books® and design are registered trademarks of
Random House Value Publishing, Inc.

Random House
New York • Toronto • London • Sydney • Auckland
http://www.randomhouse.com/

Printed and bound in China

A CIP catalogue record for this book is available from the Library of Congress.

ISBN 0-517-16075-7

8 7 6 5 4 3 2 1

Page One Photo:
Immigrants aboard a ship docking at Ellis Island in New York Harbor, circa 1908.

Page Two Photo:
*The towers of the main building at Ellis Island still stand, overlooking the place where 12
million persons arrived as immigrants into the United States between 1892 1ns 1954.*

Picture Credits:

Department of Defense: 118, 119, 120, 121
Department of the Interior: 6, 34, 35, 38, 39, 40, 41, 48, 54, 59, 68, 71
Department of Justice: 74, 87, 88, 92, 93, 96
Library of Congress: 8, 20, 21, 27, 42 (bottom), 43 (both), 44 (bottom), 45 (both), 46 (both),
47 (both), 49, 50, 51, 55, 58, 62, 63, 66 (both), 67, 76, 77, 78, 79, 80, 81, 82 (both), 83 (both),
84, 85, 89
National Archives: 1, 9, 32, 33, 36, 37, 72, 73, 75
Western History Museum: 12-14, 16-19, 22, 25, 26 28-31, 42 (top), 44 (top)
©Azia Yenne: 90, 130, 131, 139
©Bill Yenne: 2, 7, 10, 11, 15, 68-69, 91, 97-117, 124-129, 132-133, 144

Table of Contents

INTRODUCTION

Give me your tired, your poor
Your huddled masses yearning to breathe free.
The wretched refuse of your teeming shore.
Send these, the homeless, the tempest-tosst to me,
I lift my lamp beside the golden door!

— Emma Lazarus
(Inscription on the Statue of Liberty)

Above: Young immigrant children eyeing the Manhattan skyline from Ellis Island in New York Harbor.

Opposite: The Statue of Liberty has been a beacon for immigrants since 1886.

The Statue of Liberty has stood for more than a century as a beacon to the millions who passed by her in their crowded immigrant ships bound for nearby Ellis Island and a new life in a land of promise. The United States of America is a nation of immigrants. Over 95 percent of Americans are descended from people that didn't live on this continent in the eighteenth century, and nearly 10 percent of current American citizens were not born in the United States.

What we call the "great wave" of immigration in the early twentieth century is only one of a series of waves that have populated the United States with representatives of nearly every race on the face of the Earth. Each race, in turn, grafted on to the developing America a layer of its unique social customs, ideas and cultures.

Since the founding of the United States, immigration has been an important element in American history, for it has been the factor which has defined the American nationality. There have been several important waves of immigration, including that of the 1840s, that of the last decades of the twentieth century, and the previously mentioned "great wave" of immigration. This was what was referred to for many years as the "melting pot."

Early waves of immigration in the seventeenth and eighteenth centuries were characterized by northern European, primarily English, people who sought religious freedom. After the Revolutionary War, people came from Europe in search of political freedom, and as the seemingly endless promise of the new lands in the West were opened for settlement, immigrants came for the promise of economic opportunity.

In the nineteenth century, many people came from Europe to escape hardship at home. In the late 1840s, the Potato Famine in Ireland and political upheaval in Italy and Germany brought waves of immigration that began to change the ethnic makeup of America. In the 1860s, large numbers of Chinese immigrated to the West Coast, and many stayed. The melting pot was born.

From 1820 (when the United States government first began to keep official records) through 1996, the United States welcomed 63 million immigrants. Of these, 38 million arrived from Europe, 11 million from Latin America, and 7.9 million from Asia. Among the Europeans, the largest nationality group was the Germans with 7.2 million, followed by 5.4 million Italians, 5.3 million people from

England and Scotland, 5 million Irish, 4.4 million from the former Austro-Hungarian Empire (which collapsed in 1918), 3.7 million Russians and 1.3 million Swedes.

The two nations adjacent to the United States have also contributed large numbers, with 5.5 million Mexicans immigrating into the United States — most of them after 1970 — and 4.4 million Canadians arriving, primarily between 1911 and 1930. From elsewhere in the world, the United States has welcomed 1.4 million Filipinos and 1.2 million Chinese.

In one relatively brief period, between 1880 and 1920, more than 20 million Europeans — including many from eastern Europe — fled difficult conditions at home to find a new life in "the Land of Opportunity." Since 1960, the tide of immigration has been renewed, this time with new faces from Asia and Latin America.

Between 1820 and 1930, the United States would open its doors to 37 million immigrants, a number nearly as great as the population of France in 1930.

They recast the old American nation into a new image. Even as the economic conditions of the Great Depression drove the United States to close the gate, the outstanding facts in the history of United States immigration are the essential bedrock of United States national life. We would have been limited in national character and leadership, had we been all New England Puritans or Virginia Cavaliers. We needed immigrants with genius, enterprise, and loyalty to mold the United States into what it is.

This book is the history of the American immigrants: Who they are, why they came, how they got here and what they found.

THE EARLY YEARS

The first immigrants into North America were not from Europe. The ancestors of the people we now refer to as Native Americans arrived from Asia by way of the Bering Land Bridge roughly 25,000 years ago. Waves of internal immigration followed, as various groups superseded others. For example, in about 1300, the Navajo people immigrated into the American Southwest, replacing the Anasazi people who had been there for centuries before. For the purpose of this book, however, we will trace the history of immigration from the beginning of the United States as a nation through the arrival of the people from other parts of the globe since the eighteenth century.

The New World

The first Europeans to establish permanent settlements in what is now the United States were the English. By the fact of England having sent many more colonists during the seventeenth century than the other countries, the English established a body of population which imposed its language, form of government, and opportunities for individual advancement upon all later nationalities.

In 1607, the English entrepreneur Captain John Smith founded his settlement at Jamestown (named for King James I) in the territory of Virginia. The colony nearly failed several times, but the colonists held on, and in 1619 the people of Jamestown inaugurated the first representative assembly in North America, a precursor to the form of government that would later predominate. Another settlement was established at Plymouth in 1620 in what is now Massachusetts, by a group of British subjects who called themselves the Pilgrims. Fleeing what they perceived as political persecution of their religious sect, the Pilgrims came to America in their ship the *Mayflower* to establish a colony in which they could worship as they wished without governmental interference. Plymouth was important because it was the first successful North American settlement founded by ordinary Europeans without a charter from a European government.

Below: A home in Williamsburg in the former English colony of Virginia. The English were among the first immigrants to America.

Opposite: The restored House of Burgesses (legislature) in Williamsburg still flies Britain's Union Jack.

Below: Seventeenth century Dutch immigrants rest by the hearth of their home in New Amsterdam. The Dutch were among the first European immigrants to America, although they were outnumbered by the French, Spanish and English.

After Plymouth, the settlements on the Merrimac River were the oldest in all New England. In 1622, the area between the Merrimac and Kennebec Rivers, reaching from the Atlantic to the St. Lawrence, was granted by the Council of Plymouth to Sir Ferdinand Gorges and John Mason. In the spring of 1623, two small groups of emigrants were sent out by Mason and Gorges to survey the area, which was explored as early as 1614 by John Smith. The progress of the colony, however, was slow and the first villages were no more than fishing stations. After six years, the proprietors divided their dominion between them, Gorges taking the northern and Mason the southern portion of the province. In turn, John Wheelwright purchased the rights to the territory occupied by Mason's colony. A second patent was issued to the proprietor, and the name of the province was changed from Laconia to New Hampshire.

In New England, 20,000 English immigrants arrived during the first generation (1620-1642), and all through the seventeenth century, the English supplied most of the new population of America. Meanwhile, English Quakers settled Pennsylvania and English Roman Catholics founded Maryland. Since it was a crime to be a Roman Catholic in England at the time of Lord Baltimore, he and his Catholic friends founded the colony of Maryland as a refuge. Remembering their own persecutions, these Catholic liberals welcomed members of every faith, not excluding Muslims or even persons who professed no faith at all. It was not long, however, before opposition forces wrested this territory from the control of the Catholics and excluded every Catholic immigrant from the colony.

Meanwhile, in 1619, the Dutch had established a foothold with the colony of New Amsterdam near the mouth of the Hudson River (which was sold to the English in 1644), and the French arrived in what is now eastern Canada and in the Mississippi River country to the west. The first recorded immigration of Jewish people was to a Dutch colony. Driven out of Brazil by the Portuguese, these Jews were received by the Dutch government of New Amsterdam. From that day on, they have continued to represent one of the most important ethnic groups in the great and diverse city that became New York.

The French had obtained a footing in Nova Scotia and on the banks of the St. Lawrence. The English had colonized the country around Massachusetts Bay. The Dutch had established themselves on Manhattan Island and in detached settlements along the Hudson and the Delaware. Inland from Chesapeake Bay, Jamestown was so well founded as to remove all doubt of its permanency. A second wave of French immigration was composed chiefly of the French Protestant exiles called Huguenots who came after the Revocation of the Edict of Nantes in 1685. These people were primarily manufacturers and merchants.

In Florida, the Spanish had succeeded in establishing St. Augustine and several other successful settlements. Far to the west, Santa Fe was the northern outpost of Spanish influence in the heart of the continent, but the Spanish-speaking peoples were not to be a significant population within the United States until the twentieth century.

Beyond the lure of adventure and the wonder of new sights in a new land that was shared by all, each of the European powers viewed the economic development of North America in a different way. The English came primari-

ly to establish a permanent presence on the land itself. The Dutch came as traders. The Spanish came for gold. The French came for gold, but discovered wealth in furs. While the Spanish searched the Southwest for gold mines, the French explored the St. Lawrence River and the Great Lakes country in order to build and maintain a steady stream of beaver pelts to Europe.

Beavers were plentiful in the area around the Great Lakes and the St. Lawrence River, and the French discovered that their fur was of a high quality. In the course of this effort during the seventeenth century, French trappers and traders reached deeper into the heart of what is now the United States than any other nationality.

If we define "immigrants" as those who arrived in the original permanent colonies after they were established with internal forms of government, then we can say that the first immigrants were of the same nationality as the original colonists, i.e. English, Dutch and French. From the beginning of the eighteenth century, when the crowns of Scotland and England were unified, this group would also include a large number of people from Scotland. The

Germans began coming at the end of the seventeenth century. German Quakers and Pietists, answering William Penn's advertising, came to join his colony in Pennsylvania. At the beginning of the eighteenth century, when Louis XIV overran the Palatinate, thousands of Germans fled to England and were encouraged by the English government to migrate to America. The descendants of these people came to be called the "Pennsylvania Dutch," which was actually a misspelling of "Pennsylvania Deutsche." The German population soon spread out from Pennsylvania, north to New York and south to Virginia.

The eighteenth century immigration of the Scotch-Irish and Germans was a combined migration possibly as great as that of the English in the seventeenth century. Since the seaboard was already occupied, they had to move on into the continent, become frontiersmen, and wrest their living directly from the soil as the first coastal settlers had done before them. The New Englanders did not welcome them, and they settled largely in Pennsylvania, in the foothill regions of Virginia and North and South Carolina, and in Ohio, Kentucky, and Tennessee.

Above: English colonists in Massachusetts watch as the immigrant ship that brought them to America sets sail for England. Many early English immigrants arrived to settle in colonies that promised religious freedom. The early English Protestants who arrived in Massachusetts in the seventeenth and eighteenth centuries were followed in the nineteenth and twentieth by Catholics from Ireland, Italy and Portugal.

A Nation of Immigrants

The United States was born as a nation in 1783 with the end of the War of Independence and its recognition by England as an independent country. Yet the United States was still an English nation in terms of its language, ethnicity, and customs. At the time of the first census in 1790, the population of the United States — excluding Native Americans, who were not counted in the census at that time — stood at 3,929,214. Most of these people were either immigrants or descendants of relatively recent immigrants. Over 90 percent were of English or Scotch origin, and roughly seven percent were German or "Pennsylvania Deutsche."

In the early days after the independence of the United States, immigrants were welcomed by the American-born, who were themselves children of immigrants. Indeed, George Washington proclaimed in 1783 that the "bosom of America is open to receive not only the opulent and respectable stranger, but the oppressed and persecuted of all nations and religions, whom we shall welcome to a participation of all our rights and privileges."

Immigration to the United States was virtually unrestricted by official legislation, and it would continue as such for eight decades. There were, however, several acts of Congress that are an important part of the immigration history of the United States. On March 26, 1790, Congress passed, and President Washington signed, the first official *federal* act regulating immigration.

Prior to that time, immigration had been an activity that was under the control of the individual states. The act of March 26, 1790 specifically established a uniform rule for naturalization by setting the residence requirement at two years. However, an official act passed by the United States Congress on January 29, 1795, repealed the 1790 act, raised the residence requirement to five years, and required a declaration of intention to seek citizenship at least three years before they would become naturalized.

Three years later, Congress passed and President John Adams signed the Naturalization Act of June 18, 1798, which provided that clerks of the courts must furnish information about each record of naturalization to the Secretary of State. It also required — for the first

time — the registry of each alien residing in the United States at that time, as well as those arriving thereafter, and it raised the residence requirement for naturalization to a term of 14 years.

At the same time, Congress was at work on the Aliens Act of 1798, which was enacted on June 25, 1798. This was the first national attempt to regulate immigration. One of what would be known as the Alien and Sedition Acts, the Aliens Act represented the first federal law pertinent to immigration rather than naturalization. Among its provisions, it authorized the President to arrest and/or deport any alien whom he deemed dangerous to the United States. It also required the captain of any vessel to report the arrival of aliens on board such vessel to the Collector, or other chief officer, of the Customs of the Port. The deportations soon ended because the law was open to political abuse. It expired in 1800 after its two-year term, but it shows that immigration policy has been a political issue since the nation's founding.

While the Aliens Act expired without having been actively enforced, the summer of 1798 also saw the passage of the Alien Enemy Act of July 6, 1798, which would remain a permanent part of the American federal legal code. The Alien Enemy Act provided that in the case of declared war or invasion the President would have the power to restrain or remove alien enemy males of fourteen years and upwards, but with due protection of their property rights as stipulated by treaty.

The first Congress had enacted rules regarding citizenship in 1790, and from then until 1802 established the United States' early naturalization procedure. The Naturalization Act of April 14, 1802 amended and superseded provisions of the Naturalization Act of June 18, 1798, reducing the residence period for naturalization from 14 to five years. The Naturalization Act of April 14, 1802 also established basic requirements for naturalization, including good moral character, allegiance to the Constitution, a formal declaration of intention, and witnesses.

Federal and selected state courts carried out naturalization and granted citizenship as they do today, though naturalization requirements have been modified over the years.

Opposition to immigration and restrictive immigration laws have concurrent histories. The opposition to immigration began earlier than is generally known. Thomas Jefferson expressed the fear that too many sub-

Above: A drum and bugle corps performs in the restored English colonial city of Williamsburg. The flag seen flying here is actually the Grand Union Flag adopted by the united colonies in 1776. The British Union Jack was officially replaced in the corner by a blue field and white stars in 1777.

jects of the European monarchs might "pollute United States democracy" and so destroy the foundations of the United States republic. He would admit intelligent artisans, trained to some craft, since the United States might need their help. It was the peasantry he feared, and the common laborers from the crowded cities of Europe.

Few Americans in the time of Jefferson saw the matter as he did. So long as the United States had an abundance of free land open to settlement, the American people gave all immigrants a royal welcome. The lonely settler on the frontier wanted neighbors. He who had lands to sell wished as many purchasers as the world might offer. All forms of business enterprise sought to increase the home market for goods, and the United States grew at a pace which never ceased to astonish those left behind in Europe.

Immigration in the Early Nineteenth Century

As the nation grew, and immigrants and their children pushed west, open immigration continued. The majority of Americans had always welcomed immi-grants, so they simply continued to do so. They came to the United States for a variety of reasons, among them war, unemployment, and famine.

These factors worked to push people, most of them rural farmers, out of their countries. The ability to get cheap, fertile, new land worked to pull them to America. The United States possessed unlimited opportunities for development. The optimistic theory was that every honest man could make a good living, and that any clever man could, if he wished, amass wealth.

The Germans were welcomed, and the French, though they spoke no English. Quakers, who were persecuted in New England, received as their own the great rich province of Pennsylvania. When the English took over New York from the Dutch in the middle of the seventeenth century, they heard scores of languages in public houses and on the streets. All that was asked of any foreigner was that he pay his own way with work or money.

In 1820, the first year for which records were kept by the United States government, there were a total of 8,385 immigrants into the United States. Of these, 3,614 arrived from Ireland and 2,410 arrived from

England and Scotland. There were 968 from Germany, 371 from France and 209 from Canada. Between the years of 1821 and 1830, a total of 143,439 immigrants entered the United States. The largest nationality group were the 50,724 who arrived from Ireland, followed by 25,079 who arrived from England and Scotland, 8,497 who arrived from France and 6,761 who immigrated from Germany.

Until 1880, immigrants from the United Kingdom — including England and Scotland, as well as Ireland — accounted for over half of all immigrants. For most of the nineteenth century, Germans would account for roughly a third of all immigrants.

As the United States approached the third decade of the nineteenth century, a substantial flow of European immigrants began to enter the country. Many of these new immigrants arrived through the major ports of Boston and New York, and many of the poorer ones arrived in "steerage." This term applied to the inexpensive — and often windowless — passenger accommodations in the lower part of

a ship near the rudder, where the ship was steered. The first federal immigration legislation in nearly two decades specifically addressed the conditions of immigrants who traveled in steerage.

Signed into law by President James Monroe, the Steerage Act of March 2, 1819 is recalled as being the first *significant* federal law relating to immigration. Its provisions dealt with conditions of food and overcrowding by setting specific sustenance rules for passengers of ships leaving United States ports for Europe, and it set limitations on the number of passengers on all vessels either coming to or leaving the United States. The Steerage Act of March 2, 1819 also established the continuing reporting of immigration to the United States by requiring that passenger lists or manifests of all arriving vessels be delivered to the local Collector of Customs, copies transmitted to the Secretary of State, and the information reported to Congress.

With the 1819 Steerage Act, Congress had *supported* immigration by setting stan-

Above: Ships in heavy weather on the high seas. Early European immigrants faced a long and typically dangerous crossing of the North Atlantic.

dards for conditions on passenger vessels coming into United States ports. Still, unlimited immigration was not always favored by all Americans. From time to time, mainly during times of economic decline, there were efforts to slow the tide of immigration.

Unhappy with delays in federal action, some states passed local laws governing the entry of immigrants. Later, United States Supreme Court decisions of 1849 and 1875 declared all such state laws unconstitutional. The court interpreted them as attempts to regulate foreign commerce, a function that belongs to the federal government alone. The 1819 Steerage Acts regarding travel on sailing ships also ordered that ship captains provide port officials with passenger lists, or manifests. These ships' manifests formed the first formal immigration records. The records soon revealed patterns among early nineteenth century immigrants to the United States.

Five years later, the official act passed by the United States Congress, and signed into law by President Monroe on May 26, 1824, facilitated the naturalization of certain aliens

who had entered the United States as minors, by setting a two-year instead of a three-year interval between declaration of intention and admission to citizenship.

President Monroe is also remembered for his Monroe Doctrine, which was contained in his annual message to Congress on December 2, 1823, and in which he outlined three essential points that in later years became a cardinal doctrine of United States foreign policy and relations with the rest of the world in terms of citizenship. Monroe stated that "The American continents, by the free and independent condition which they have assumed and maintain, are henceforth not to be considered as subjects for future colonization by any European powers . . . . We should consider any attempt [by European powers] to extend their system to any portion of this hemisphere as dangerous to our peace and safety."

Through the Monroe Doctrine, the United States defined its own sovereignty in relation to the aspirations of the European powers and encouraged the citizens of those powers "yearning to breathe free" to emigrate to America. While it was much later interpreted as an American effort to dominate the Western Hemisphere politically, it was much more of an effort toward pulling the Western Hemisphere from under the European shadow.

Between the years of 1831 and 1840, a total of 599,125 immigrants entered the United States. The largest nationality group were the 207,381 who arrived from Ireland, followed by 152,454 who arrived from Germany, 75,810 who arrived from England and Scotland and 45,575 who immigrated from France.

In terms of United States federal legislation on immigration, conditions on ships were governed solely by the Steerage Act of March 2, 1819 and prior legislation for nearly a quarter of the nineteenth century. This was until the passage of the official Passenger Acts passed by the United States Congress, signed into law by President Zachary Taylor on February 22, 1847.

This legislation provided specific regulations to safeguard passengers on merchant vessels. It was subsequently amended by the act of March 2, 1847, which expanded the allowance of passenger space. Eight years later, as the storm clouds of the American Civil War had begun to gather, Congress passed and President Franklin Pierce signed, the Passenger Act of March 3, 1855. It essentially repealed the Passenger Acts of 1847 and combined their provisions in a codified form. The 1855 law

reaffirmed the duty of the captain of any vessel to report the arrival of alien passengers. It also established separate reporting to the Secretary of State distinguishing permanent and temporary immigration.

In 1855, Castle Garden in New York Harbor had become what was probably the first full-time immigration station in the United States. It was maintained by the government of the state of New York rather than the United States government. Eventually it would pass nine million immigrants into America under the supervision of the State of New York, but it also had a colorful background before it became an immigrant station.

It is a coincidence that Castle Garden was first built as a fort by the United States federal government. Erected in 1807 and called Castle Clinton, it was manned by soldiers through the War of 1812 and owned by the United States until 1822, at which time it was

ceded to the city of New York. About two years later it was leased to private interests and became a place of amusement at which P.T. Barnum's circus often entertained. After 1839, Castle Garden came into prominence as a beautiful and fashionable resort. After being closed for renovations in the latter part of 1846 and spring of 1847, the Garden reopened. The outstanding event, and one for which old Castle Garden will ever be famous, was the triumph of Jenny Lind, the Swedish Nightingale.

P.T. Barnum was her manager. And what a success she scored! After her first concert, the demand for seats was phenomenal. The takings of the farewell night were over $16,000. Afterward, an Italian opera company reigned for a season at Castle Garden.

In 1855, with the establishment of Castle Garden as an immigration station under the supervision of the State of New York, things began to happen. The facilities were

Above: Many immigrants to America from Ireland began their journey from docks along the River Liffey, which runs through the city of Dublin.

inadequate for the proper care and treatment of the immigrants who had begun to arrive in flood-tide numbers. The German revolution of 1848 had started an exodus from that country, while the Irish and Scandinavian peoples were also joining the caravan.

Hospital patients from Castle Garden were detained at Ward's Island in the East River. At Ward's Island, riots frequently occurred. Many immigrants escaped by swimming to the Manhattan shore, asking to be arrested and confined in the New York jails, rather than remain at Ward's Island with the insane and, some charged, in a state of starvation. On one occasion, an investigation revealed the startling fact that the bodies of dead immigrants were being used in medical schools.

Other European Ethnic Groups

In the 13 colonies that rebelled against England in 1776, beginning the course of events that led to the establishment of the United States, the Anglo-Scottish ethnic group was the overwhelming majority. However, with the beginning of the nineteenth century, new waves of Germans and Irish began to arrive.

The Germans who came in the early nineteenth century were educated liberals fleeing the despotic government of their country. Many of them were forced out of Germany after the revolution of 1848, in which they took a leading part. They sprang largely from the middle classes of Germany. Later, several severe industrial depressions urged the peasants, too, to emigrate, and many would come during the years from 1873 to 1879.

America has always appreciated the underdog. In the early nineteenth century, immigrants who reminded Americans of their fight — as underdogs — against the British Empire were welcomed. The Irish were generally liked because they had fought the British tyrant through the cen-

turies. The "Forty-Eighters" from all countries in Europe were welcomed, as they were refugees from the great wave of revolutions in 1848 that sought to establish American-style democracy in Europe. If the newcomers were Protestants, they found a pew awaiting them in any American church. If they were Jews, the Americans remembered that they had been subjected to Russian tyranny. If the immigrant had no religion at all, his position was amply protected by the Constitution and the laws. America's generous treatment of new arrivals became proverbial, and it was a source of wonder and admiration to the common people of Europe.

In 1846, when a fungus attacked the potato crop in Ireland, it touched off several years of horrible starvation that would result in over a million deaths.

Because the potato was the staple food of the Irish diet, and because a vast majority of the crop was obliterated for three years in a row, the Famine in Ireland was a disaster unparalleled in modern European history. So many people either died or left Ireland that that island nation has never recovered its 1840 population. The Irish Potato Famine of the 1840s was also the catalyst for the mass migration that would lead to what remains one of the largest ethnic groups in the United States.

Between the years of 1841 and 1850, a total of 1,713,251 immigrants entered the United States. The largest nationality group were the 780,719 who arrived from Ireland in the wake of the Famine, followed by 434,626 who arrived from Germany, 267,044 who arrived from England and Scotland, and 77,262 who immigrated from France.

While Irish immigration dominated the 1840s because of the Famine, during the 1850s, the Germans would move to the fore because of turmoil in the German-speaking principalities of central Europe that increased after the 1848 upheaval.

Between the years of 1851 and 1860, a total of 2,598,214 immigrants entered the United States. The largest nationality group were the 951,667 who arrived from Germany, closely followed by 914,119 immigrants from Ireland, 423,974 who arrived from England and Scotland, and 76,358 who immigrated from France. The peak year was 1854, in which 427,833 persons immigrated. It was, in fact, the only year between 1820 and 1880 to top 400,000. The annual totals in the late 1850s were below 200,000 immigrants.

The Civil War Era

The Civil War was perhaps the most difficult turning point in American history, and an important one in terms of defining the United States as a nation, and indeed as a single unified nation.

The war lasted for four years and it included some of the bloodiest military campaigns in history.

The war had its roots in regional differences — including ideas regarding slavery — that came to a head in the 1850s. By 1860, political attitudes about slavery had hardened, and the Southern economy seemed strong, as it was a leading international supplier of cotton, while the North was in the throes of the Recession of 1857. In terms of immigration, the Civil War era was marked by a major surge of new arrivals into the states of the North, as industry expanded to meet the needs of the war effort and people came from Europe for job opportunities. A large number of immigrants — especially those from Ireland, Italy, and Germany — enlisted in the Union Army. The Union commander, General Ulysses S. Grant, entering Richmond after the retreat of Confederate General Robert E. Lee, was accompanied by a

cavalry brigade composed of African Americans under an Italian-American commander. Between the years of 1861 and 1870 — the decade that included the Civil War — a total of 2,314,824 immigrants entered the United States. The largest nationality group were the 787,486 who arrived from Germany, followed by 606,896 who arrived from England and Scotland, 435,778 who arrived from Ireland, and 153,878 who immigrated from Canada.

The years of the Civil War were also, of course, marked by major progress in eliminating slavery and incorporating the African American population into the larger population. In terms of immigration policy, the United States Congress made its first attempt to centralize control of these procedures during the Civil War. An official act passed by the United States Congress, and signed into law by President Abraham Lincoln on July 4, 1864, provided for a Commissioner of Immigration to be appointed by the President to serve under the authority of the Secretary of State. The law also authorized immigrant labor contracts whereby would-be immigrants would pledge their wages to pay for transportation. However, on March 30, 1868, the Act of July 4, 1864 would be repealed.

Above: Many immigrants served with the Union Army during the Civil War. Seen here at Harrison's Landing, Virginia in July 1862 are a group of men from the Irish Brigade . This unit saw service throughout the main eastern theater of the war, especially in the Peninsular Campaign of May-August 1862.

FORCED IMMIGRATION

Below: African slave traders taking other Africans to be sold into slavery on the western coast of the continent, circa 1800.

Opposite: An "Auction & Negro Sales" establishment on Whitehall Street in Atlanta as photographed by George Barnard after the city was captured by Union Army troops in 1864 during the Civil War.

Coincidental with these major voluntary migrations is one chapter in American population history which is so terrible that the conventional nineteenth and early twentieth century historians usually passed it by with only a sidelong glance. Slavery has existed throughout human history. The pyramids of Egypt were built by slaves. Even the Bible itself is filled with stories of people being sold into slavery. The great Greek and Roman civilizations that we hold as the foundations of modern European civilization kept slaves, and so did the Native American civilizations that were encountered by Europeans who came to the Americas.

The Slave Trade

Today we still tend to ignore the slaving practice of most historic cultures, but at least we have begun to come to grips with slavery practiced by the seventeenth through nineteenth century landowners in what is now the eastern part of the United States. The importation of West African people into the Caribbean and what is now the eastern United States began in the early seventeenth century, when Portuguese traders exploring the coast of Africa began trading for slaves with African slave traders who had been engaged in the practice for centuries. It was a curious situation of black Africans trading other — less fortunate — black Africans to white Europeans for merchandise such as weapons, ammunition, metal, liquor, trinkets, and cloth.

During the seventeenth century, the slave trade was controlled by the West Africans themselves, who sold people into slavery, and by the Dutch, who transported the slaves across the Atlantic. However, the Treaty of Utrecht, in 1714, gave a monopoly of the slave trade to the British and their American colonists. Colonial and British merchants turned West Indian sugar into rum, and then traded the liquor on the coasts of Africa for human beings. Chained into the holds of ships in hor-

rible — and often deadly — conditions, the slaves were carried across the Atlantic to the Western Hemisphere. Here they were much in demand in labor intensive agriculture such as sugar cane plantations in the Caribbean, and cotton fields in what would become the southern United States.

Between the sixteenth and the nineteenth centuries, an estimated eight million to 15 million Africans reached the Western Hemisphere, with about six million "immigrating" in the eighteenth century alone.

Organized opposition to slavery began with the Society of Friends (the Quakers), who voiced their opinions publicly as of about 1724. As there was opposition to slavery, there was also a vocal opposition to the slave trade itself. There was a movement against the importation of slaves because, in part, the government of King George III was accused of assisting in the nefarious traffic and profiting by it. In 1774, Rhode Island became the first colony to abolish slavery, although the United States government, in 1788, provided that the slave trade could continue for 20 years because of its economic importance in the South.

Abolition and Emancipation

The slave trade was officially abolished on March 2, 1807, when Congress passed a law prohibiting the importation of slaves from Africa as of January 1, 1808. Responsibility for enforcement shifted among several agencies, and the enforcement provisions themselves were ineffective. A number of attempts were made to strengthen these

provisions, but none were successful. Slavery remained legal in the South, and despite the ban on importation of slaves, they continued to be bought and sold in the United States.

Meanwhile, the abolitionist movement gathered momentum in the northern states. By the 1830s, William Lloyd Garrison was publishing the abolitionist newspaper *The Liberator* and the American Anti-Slavery Society had been formed in Philadelphia. In the 1840s, the Underground Railroad was active in helping slaves escape to the North, to freedom. As the tide of protest to slavery mounted, the United States was headed toward the Civil War. In his speech accepting the Republican presidential nomination in 1860, Abraham Lincoln said that "The nation could not survive half-slave and half-free."

Within a year, the Civil War had begun. On September 22, 1862, as the war still raged, Lincoln issued the Emancipation Proclamation, which stated "That on the 1st day of January, AD 1863, all persons held as slaves within any State or designated part of a State the people whereof shall then be in rebellion against the United States shall be then, thenceforward, and forever free; and the executive government of the United States, including the military and naval authority thereof, will recognize and maintain the freedom of such persons and will do no act or acts to repress such persons, or any of them, in any efforts they may make for their actual freedom.

"That the executive will on the 1st day of January aforesaid, by proclamation, designate the States and parts of States, if any, in which the people thereof, respectively, shall then be in rebellion against the United States; and the fact that any State or the people thereof shall on that day be in good faith represented in the Congress of the United States by members chosen thereto at elections wherein a majority of the qualified voters of such States shall have participated shall, in the absence of strong countervailing testimony, be deemed conclusive evidence that such State and the people thereof are not then in rebellion against the United States."

Lincoln declared that all persons held as slaves within most of the Confederacy were to be freed. Meanwhile, Congress passed and sent to the states the thirteenth amendment to the Constitution of the United States. It was proposed to the legislatures at the 38th Congress on January 31, 1865, and was declared in December to have been ratified by the legislatures of 27 of the 36 states. The

thirteenth amendment stated that "Neither slavery nor involuntary servitude, except as a punishment for crime whereof the party shall have been duly convicted, shall exist within the United States, or any place subject to their jurisdiction."

The thirteenth amendment was ratified by Illinois on February 1, 1865, by Rhode Island on February 2, by Michigan on February 2, by Maryland on February 3, by New York on February 3, by Pennsylvania on February 3, by West Virginia on February 3, by Missouri on February 6, by Maine on February 7, by Kansas on February 7, by Massachusetts on February 7, by Virginia on February 9, by Ohio on February 10, by Indiana on February 13, by Nevada on February 16, by Louisiana on February 17, by Minnesota on February 23, by Wisconsin on February 24, by Vermont on March 9, by Tennessee on April 7, by Arkansas on April 14, by Connecticut on May 4, by New Hampshire on July 1, by South Carolina on November 13, by Alabama on December 2, by North Carolina on December 4, and by Georgia on December 6, 1865.

The ratification process was completed on December 6, 1865, but the amendment was subsequently ratified by Oregon on December 8, by California on December 19, by Florida on December 28, 1865 (Florida again ratified on June 9 in 1868, upon its adoption of a new constitution), by Iowa on January 15, 1866, by New Jersey on January 23, 1866 (after having rejected the amendment on March 16, 1865), by Texas on February 18, 1870, by Delaware, February 12, 1901 (after having rejected the amendment on February 8, 1865), by Kentucky on March 18, 1976 (after having rejected it on February 24 in 1865). The amendment was rejected (and not subsequently ratified) by Mississippi on December 4.

The Naturalization Act of 1870, passed by the United States Congress and signed into law by President Ulysses S. Grant on July 14, 1870 not only established a system of controls on the naturalization process and penalties for fraudulent practices, it extended the naturalization laws to include all aliens of African birth, as well as those persons of African descent.

Above: A congregation in an African American church in the late nineteenth century after the abolition of slavery and the freeing of the slaves.

THE
MELTING POT

By the census of 1860, the population of the United States — excluding slaves and Native Americans — stood at 31,443,321. Between that year and 1880, immigration surged to eight million arrivals, with more than nine out of 10 of the immigrants coming from northern and western Europe, especially Germany, Scandinavia, and the British Isles.

The first immigration office in the federal government was created in 1864 by a law intended to encourage immigration. Under this law, the President appointed a commissioner of immigration within the State Department to regulate the transportation and settlement of "emigrants," but the law had no effect on the commissions, boards, or other officers who were responsible for immigration in each of the states. The commissioner's office was abolished when the law was repealed four years later. Other federal laws were passed in the 1880s to prevent the admission of undesirable aliens and to control contract labor, but authority over immigration, including enforcement of the federal statutes, remained at the state level. At the same time, the number of immigrants coming into America was rising rapidly.

Between the years of 1871 and 1880, a total of 2,812,191 immigrants entered the United States. The largest nationality group were the 718,182 who arrived from Germany, followed by 548,043 who arrived from England and Scotland, 436,871 who arrived from Ireland and 383,640 who immigrated from Canada.

Germany continued in the forefront during the following decade, as a total of 5,246,613 immigrants entered the United States between the years of 1881 and 1890, nearly twice as many as during the preceding decade. The largest nationality group were the 1,452,970 who arrived from Germany, followed by 807,357 who arrived from England and Scotland, 655,482 who arrived from Ireland, and 393,304 who immigrated from Canada. Also significant were 391,776 immigrants from Sweden.

By the 1890s, however, immigrants began to arrive from countries on the southern and eastern rim of Europe and, in a little more than 10 years, they represented the majority of immigrants. At this point, the United States had started to become the true "melting pot" of the world.

The New Demographics

Among the ethnic groups that began to arrive in large numbers during this period were the Italians, the Hungarians and others from the Austro-Hungarian Empire, the Scandinavians, the Eastern European Jews, the Slavic people from the Balkans, the Poles and the Russians. Able to earn only a few cents a day as workers on their native farms and in the mines, they hastened to the United States, where wages were at least $1.50 a day. They all had brought with them ancient traditions and cultures whose contribution would be important to the evolution of American civilization.

Industrialization caused changes in the type of people moving to America. Unskilled or general laborers now dominated the workers coming from Britain and elsewhere

Below: A pair of Italian immigrants from the island of Sardinia, circa 1865.

Opposite: A family of Italian immigrants. The older children brought their musical instruments.

Below: An Albanian immigrant woman in traditional costume, circa 1870. By this time, immigration from the eastern Mediterranean area was on the increase.

in northern Europe. In the years after 1840 this category of immigrants had risen by 20 percent over prior decades. More of them came to the United States from European cities than before, and less from European farms. Many of the immigrants moved to the growing American cities and towns where industrialization in the New World created a constant demand for labor. Industrial growth even made transatlantic travel easier. The telegraph and steam-powered ships running on regular schedules both worked to create a reliable transportation system. Certain cities, especially port cities such as New Orleans, New York, and San Francisco, have always been more like melting pots than other places.

While Germany, Ireland, and Britain still provided most of the immigrants to the United States from 1860 until about 1880, growing numbers came from Scandinavia, China, and South America. Factors that pushed immigrants from their homes, factors that pulled them to America, and better transportation explain this shift in immigration patterns. For example, Norwegians suffered a long economic slump from 1866 to 1870 and Chinese in the Canton region faced famine.

Both events caused major migrations to America, while economic growth in the American West pulled immigrants by creating a demand for labor. Western mines, mills, and railroads hired large numbers of Latin American, Chinese, and European immigrants. For example, nearly one third of western miners in the 1860s were Chinese, but many others came from Chile, Peru, and Mexico.

The Scandinavians had come regularly since the foundation of the United States, and during the latter nineteenth century about two million immigrants from the northern countries came to settle in every section of the United States, especially in Minnesota and the Dakotas.

The door to immigration stayed open through most of the nineteenth century because American industry was expanding and it needed workers. At one time an English shipping line made a contract with the government of Austria-Hungary calling for the delivery at continental ports of 20,000 immigrants to America annually. For this, the shipping line paid a regular stipend to the Hungarian government. That government then induced people to sell their property and leave homes where many had been comfortable and happy. In America they often found themselves in slums without jobs or other means of decent living.

Immigration based on religion was also an important factor. Just as Protestants had come from England and France in the seventeenth and eighteenth centuries to seek religious freedom, many Jews from central and eastern Europe arrived at the end of the nineteenth century.

Immigration in the Late Nineteenth Century

Throughout the nineteenth century, intensifying in the years after the American Civil War, ensuing political instability, restrictive religious laws and deteriorating economic conditions in Europe began to fuel the largest mass human migration in the history of the world.

In 1883, when Emma Lazarus wrote in her sonnet *The New Colossus* about the tired, poor and the huddled masses yearning to breathe free, she was speaking of these European immigrants that were coming into America. She jabbed cynically at the European powers when she spoke of these poor souls as "the wretched refuse of your teeming shore." Speaking to the European leaders on behalf of the Statue of Liberty, which was even then in the planning stages for an 1886 unveiling, Lazarus added "Send these, the homeless, the tempest-tosst to me, I lift my lamp beside the golden door!"

During 1882, a watershed year in the history of American immigration, the number of entries rose to an all-time annual high of 788,992, a record that would stand for 21 years. The volume of people arriving from northern and western Europe reached its peak, while that from southern and eastern Europe — including central European and Russian Jews — steadily grew.

Europe's changing economy now caused workers to move away from southern and eastern European countries, among them

Austria-Hungary, Bulgaria, Italy, Greece, Poland, Portugal, Romania, Russia, Spain, and Turkey. By the 1890s, this "new" immigration from southeastern Europe exceeded the "old" from northwestern Europe. The "new" immigrants were generally less skilled than those who came earlier.

Rapid industrial and economic growth pulled these migrants to American cities. The United States' own population simply could not meet the need for labor as industrial jobs multiplied. Even native-born, rural Americans migrated to jobs in the bigger cities as the farming frontier gave way to timberlands and desert.

Between the years of 1891 and 1900, a total of 3,687,564 immigrants entered the United States, significantly fewer than in the

previous decade. It was in the 1890s that the origin of the immigrants underwent a major shift from northern Europe to southern and central Europe and Russia. The largest nationality group were the 651,893 people who arrived from Italy, followed by 592,707 from the Austro-Hungarian Empire, 505,290 who arrived from Tsarist Russia, and 505,152 who immigrated from Germany. Ireland, which had contributed such a large number through the middle years of the century, saw only 383,416 people emigrate to the United States. However, the aggregate total for the entire United Kingdom — England, Scotland and Ireland — was 659,774.

As can be seen from this data, Italian immigration — which had first became notice-

Above: An military officer eyes potential candidates for forced conscription. In many eastern European countries in the nineteenth century, this practice served as a catalyst that caused many men to consider immigration to the United States. Ironically, many of those who immigrated between 1860 and 1865 found themselves fighting in the Civil War.

able in the 1880s with 307,309 people — soon rose to high proportions. The number of Italians increased perhaps more rapidly than immigration from any other country. Within half a century five million Italians would enter the United States.

Of course, not all of the Europeans arriving in the United States were "huddled masses." Many arrived with first and second class steamship tickets. New York was the most popular destination of steamship companies. The great steamship lines such as White Star, Red Star, Cunard, and Hamburg-America played a significant role in the history of immigration. While most immigrants entered the United States through New York — America's most important city — others sailed into many ports such as Boston, San Francisco, and Savannah.

Meanwhile, the Immigration Act of 1882 is recalled by legislative historians as being the first general United States immigration law. Signed by President Chester Arthur on August 3 of that year, the Immigration Act established a system of central control of immigration through state boards under the Secretary of the Treasury. It provided for broadened restrictions on immigration by adding to the classes of inadmissible aliens, including persons likely to become a public charge. It also introduced a tax of $.50 on each passenger brought to the United States. This tax would continually increase in small increments over the years, and it would eventually be bumped up to $4.00 by the Immigration Act of 1907.

In 1886, the year that the Statue of Liberty was unveiled, the first general United States Contract Labor Law was passed by the United States Congress, and signed into law by President Arthur on February 26. The Contract Labor Law made it unlawful to import aliens into the United States under contract for the perform-ance of labor or services of any kind. Exceptions were provided for aliens temporarily in the United States engaging other foreigners as secretaries or servants. Also exempted were actors, artists, lecturers, domestic servants, and skilled aliens working in an industry not yet established in the United States.

The Contract Labor Law of 1885 was amended through an official act passed by the United States Congress, and signed into law by President Grover Cleveland on February 23, 1887. This act amended the Contract Labor Law, rendering it enforceable by charging the Secretary of the Treasury with enforcement, which meant that prohibited persons would be sent back upon their arrival.

A few days after the amendment of the Contract Labor Law, the United States Congress passed a law which restricted the ownership of real estate — with certain specific exceptions — in the United States to American citizens and those who had lawfully declared their intention to become citizens. It was signed into law by President Cleveland on March 3, 1887.

The following year the United States Congress passed the first measure since the Aliens Act of 1798 to provide for expulsion of aliens. The Act of 1888, signed into law by President Cleveland on October 19, directed the return within one year after entry of any immigrant who had landed in violation of the Contract Labor Laws of February 26, 1885 and February 23, 1887.

In 1888, Congress established a select committee to investigate problems caused by the divided authority over immigration. It recommended consolidating this authority within a single federal agency and drafted legislation that Congress officially enacted as the Immigration Act of 1891.

Signed by President Benjamin Harrison on March 3, 1891, the law established complete and definite federal control over immigration by providing for an office of the Superintendent of Immigration under the Secretary of the Treasury. The Immigration Act of 1891 is seen by legislative historians as being the first truly comprehensive law for national control of immigration. It formally established the Bureau of Immigration under the Treasury Department to administer all immigration laws except the Chinese Exclusion Act. The Immigration Act of 1891 also further restricted immigration by adding to the inadmissible classes persons likely to become public charges, persons suffering from certain contagious diseases, felons, persons convicted of other crimes or misdemeanors, polygamists, and aliens assisted by others by payment of passage. Although it was effectively unenforceable, the Immigration Act of 1891 also forbade "the encouragement of immigration by means of advertisement."

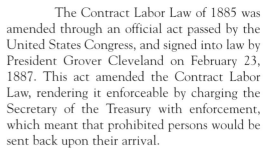

As a result of this new law, all the duties previously deferred to the states were transferred by the end of fiscal year (June 30) 1891 to United States inspection officers, and the Bureau of Immigration began operations in the Treasury Department on July 12, 1891, as the first federal immigration agency. Besides its headquarters in Washington, DC, the Bureau opened 24 inspection stations (including Ellis Island in January 1892) at ports of entry along both borders and in major seaports. The Marine Hospital Service began conducting medical inspections of arriving immigrants.

Late nineteenth century immigration law served to increase the federal government's role in regulating immigration while it reduced the duties of state governments. Later laws expanded or increased the number of "excludable classes" created by the law of 1882. The Immigration Act of 1891 excluded polygamists, persons convicted of crimes involving moral turpitude, and those suffering a "loathsome or contagious disease" — thus requiring medical examination of immigrants. The general immigration law of 1903 added epileptics, insane persons, professional beggars, and anarchists to the excludable classes. Immigrant inspectors had to inspect each incoming immigrant to see that they were qualified to enter the United States.

The 1891 law also ordered deportation for those who entered unlawfully. Another law in 1893 created boards of special inquiry to review certain cases, and required all vessels entering the United States to furnish passenger lists. Each of these new functions (inspection, deportation, case reviews, etc.) was now intended to be the specific responsibility of the federal government.

Deportation usually serves one of two purposes. Either it defends the public against crime or economic burden, as happens with

Above: A young woman from a fishing village bids farewell to family and friends before beginning the long and arduous voyage across the Atlantic to a new life in America.

Below: Eastern European immigrants in front of the main building at Ellis Island. The last years of the nineteenth century saw many people arrive in the United States from this part of the world.

criminal aliens or public charges, or it protects national security by removing subversive or disloyal aliens. In short, it is a method of expelling those who should have been excluded when inspected, who entered illegally, or who became deportable after entry.

The number of deportable classes grew along with the number of exclusions, since the two are linked. Also, national political or economic conditions influenced the focus of deportation at various times. After 1917 the bureau would focus on deporting subversives, while during the Great Depression many public charges faced deportation because they could not support themselves.

By the Immigration Act of 1891, Congress created the Office (later Bureau) of Immigration, the predecessor to today's Immigration and Naturalization Service. Before that time, a Treasury official oversaw the states' regulation of immigration to see that they complied with steerage or contract labor laws. The new law stated that a Superintendent of Immigration should enforce the law under the supervision of the Secretary of the Treasury. The new Superintendent took charge of immigration matters during the summer of 1891. Four years later, by the Act of March 2, 1895, the title of Superin-

tendent changed to Commissioner General of Immigration. In 1903, the Bureau of Immigration would be moved to the newly established Department of Commerce and Labor and given broader responsibilities.

By establishing the Bureau of Immigration, the Immigration Act allowed the Secretary of the Treasury to establish rules for inspection operations along the borders of Canada, British Columbia (which was then not yet part of Canada), and Mexico. A caveat on these inspection activities was that they were not to "obstruct or unnecessarily delay, impede, or annoy passengers in ordinary travel between these countries and the United States."

Two years later, the official act passed by the United States Congress, and signed into law by President Benjamin Harrison on March 3, 1893 added to the reporting requirements regarding alien arrivals to the United States such new information as occupation, marital status, ability to read or write, amount of money in possession, and facts regarding physical and mental health. This information was needed to determine admissibility according to the expanding list of grounds for exclusion. It also established boards of special inquiry to decide the admissibility of alien arrivals.

Although the United States federal government enacted laws regarding immigration, prior to 1890, the individual states — rather than the federal government — regulated immigration into the United States. By 1890, it had become apparent that state facilities — especially in New York City, where the majority of European immigrants landed — were ill-equipped and unprepared to handle the growing numbers of immigrants arriving yearly. Unfortunately compounding the problems of the facilities were the corruption and incompetence that were found to be common.

Under orders from President Benjamin Harrison in 1890, the federal government intervened and undertook construction of a new federally-operated immigration station on Ellis Island.

The Establishment of Ellis Island as a Processing Center

The most important port of entry in the history of immigration into the United States is a small island in New York Harbor, just off the New Jersey coast, within the shadow of the Statue of Liberty. From 1892 to 1954, over 12 million immigrants entered the United States through the portal of Ellis Island. Through the years, this gateway to the New World was enlarged from its original 3.3 acres to 27. 5 acres mostly by landfill obtained from ship ballast and possibly excess earth from the construction of the New York City subway system.

Named for one-time owner Samuel Ellis, the island had a varied history. The local Indian tribes had called it "Kiosk," or Gull Island. Due to its rich and abundant oyster beds and plentiful and profitable shad runs, it was known as Oyster Island for many generations during the Dutch and English colonial periods. By the time Samuel Ellis became the island's last private owner in the 1770s, the island had been called Kiosk, Oyster, Dyre, Bucking, and Anderson's Island. In this way, Ellis Island developed from a sandy island that barely rose above the high tide mark into a harbor fort, an ammunition and ordinance depot named Fort Gibson, and finally into an immigration station.

When the great explorer Henry Hudson landed at Ellis Island in 1609, he found Native Americans fishing from its shores and

Above: Immigrant boats docked before the main building at the Ellis Island immigration center. Boats of this type met the large, ocean-going steamers at the docks in New York City and delivered the immigrants to Ellis Island for processing.

gathered around their campfires in the background. During the sixteenth and early seventeenth centuries, in the days of Dutch Governor Peter Stuyvesant, and through the tenure of the second Dutch Governor, Wouter van Twiller, Ellis Island — then called Oyster Island — was an exclusive resort. In the seventeenth century, young Dutch boys with gleaming shoe buckles, blue pantaloons and bright doublets took their sweethearts to Oyster Island in small boats to eat roasted oysters, feasting, singing and dancing until sunset.

For almost 150 years Oyster Island continued to be New Amsterdam's favorite resort for picnics, oyster roasts, clam bakes, and fishing parties. It passed finally into the hands of Samuel Ellis, a farmer from Bergen County, New Jersey. His strange will, recorded in Abstracts of Wills in New York (1786-1796, page 325), says, among other things: "I give to the child to be born to Catherine Westervelt, if it be a son, Oyster Island, commonly known by the name of Ellis Island, with all the buildings thereon." Whether Samuel Ellis failed to pay his taxes, or the child of Catherine Westervelt was born a girl instead of a boy, or whether New York State bought the island, is not to be found in any accessible record. The island became

known as Bucking Island and passed, a few years later, into the hands of the state.

Between 1794 and 1890 Ellis Island played a mostly uneventful but still important military role in United States history. When the British had occupied New York City during the Revolutionary War, His Majesty's powerful fleet was able to sail unimpeded directly into New York Harbor, so after independence the United States government decided that a series of coastal fortifications in New York Harbor should be constructed.

After a great deal of legal disagreement over ownership of the island, the United States government finally purchased Ellis Island from New York State in 1808. Ellis Island was approved as a site for fortifications, and the United States Army constructed a parapet for three tiers of circular guns, making the island part of the new harbor defense system that included Castle Clinton at the Battery on Manhattan Island, Castle Williams on Governor's Island, Fort Wood on Bedloe's Island, and two earthworks-type forts at the entrance to New York Harbor at the Verrazano Narrows. The fort at Ellis Island was later named Fort Gibson, in honor of an officer killed during the War of 1812.

In the early spring of 1831, a notorious pirate named Gibbs was captured and brought to justice. After his trial, he was hanged on Ellis Island, which became known as Gibbet's Island. In 1841, the federal government commenced the erection of Fort Gibson, which mounted 15 guns and quartered a garrison of 80 men.

The guns of Fort Gibson remained silent during the Civil War, and by the end of the nineteenth century, the prospect of a naval invasion of New York Harbor had diminished to nonexistent.

Meanwhile, New York's importance as a port of entry led local authorities to set up an immigration processing center in New York Harbor. Castle Garden in the Battery (originally known as Castle Clinton) served as the New York State immigration station from 1855 to 1890, and approximately eight million immigrants, mostly from northern and western Europe, passed through its doors.

As noted previously, these early immigrants had come from nations such as England, Ireland, Germany, and the Scandinavian countries and constituted the first large wave of immigrants that settled and populated the United States. However, by 1890, Castle Garden was clearly obsolete and overwhelmed as a processing center, and President Benjamin Harrison ordered the federal government to take charge of the day-to-day activities of immigration processing. While the new immigration station on Ellis Island was under construction, the Barge Office at the Battery was used for the processing of immigrants.

In 1890, after the federal government assumed jurisdiction over immigration, Ellis Island was designated as an immigrant station. This was a relief to the citizens who resided near the New Jersey shore, for they had for years feared an explosion of the government powder magazine there. At first there was a demand that the immigrant station be established on Bedloe's Island, but because thousands of American citizens had donated funds for the erection of the Statue of Liberty, following its presentation to the United States by France, the reaction of the donors thwarted that plan.

Above: In the main building at Ellis Island, the Registry Room, or Great Hall, was the focal point of immigrant processing. It was here that people were told whether or not they would be allowed to enter the United States. The vast majority were granted entry.

On May 25, 1890, the United States government, having removed all guns, powder, and other munitions, formally placed Ellis Island under the supervision of the United States Treasury Department.

The new, large structure on Ellis Island was built of Georgia pine with a slate roof, and its doors opened on January 1, 1892. The first immigrant to be processed at Ellis Island was a 15-year-old girl from Ireland named Annie Moore, who was accompanied by her two brothers. Millions more were soon to follow.

A report in a New York newspaper dated April 30, 1897 stated:

"The record of recent years for the number of Irish immigrants landed at Ellis Island in any day was broken yesterday. 700 of them, mostly red-cheeked, laughing girls, were brought there from the steamers *Majestic* and *Serbia*, which arrived yesterday from Queenstown [now Cobh, near Cork].

"Of these, 65 percent of them had their passage prepaid by their friends in this country. Three-fourths of the immigrants started at once out of town, most of them going into New England states. The remainder will stay in the metropolitan district. Only some half dozen of the arrivals were debarred from landing."

During the evening of June 14, 1897, only five years after the Ellis Island Immigration Station opened, a fire burned the Georgia pine building completely to the ground. The fire was the most destructive of all the calamities which have befallen Ellis Island.

The property loss resulting from the burning of the original buildings amounted to approximately $750,000 in 1897 dollars, but fortunately, no lives were lost. The fire was discovered just after midnight, when there were about 200 persons on the island, including immigrants in the detention pen, invalids in the hospital, attendants, nurses, and watchmen. Five or six boats were always kept at the island, and by quick work all were brought to the Barge Office.

Fire boats and tugs surrounded the island as soon as the fire was discovered by the lookout of the Harbor Police Station at the Battery, but the thin streams of water they were able to furnish had slight effect upon the Georgia pine buildings. It was reported that the fire burned and spread as though the expansive landing sheds had been covered with oil, while

Above: Immigrants walking toward their ship on the large pier at the head of the main docking area at Ellis Island.

trails of fire ran along the rain gutters and spread from point to point, licking up and down the trellis work. From all parts of New York, nearby New Jersey, and Brooklyn, people gathered to view the great fire. When it was learned that the blaze was sweeping Ellis Island and that all the immigrants were safe, the comment in the crowds was said to be, "It's a great show — and after all, Uncle Sam can afford it." This flippant attitude concealed the fact that the fire was a serious disaster.

The most debilitating loss, more than the destruction of the buildings, was the burning of the records. From the immigrants' point of view, however, nothing was so important as the loss of their baggage. All the 61 immigrants awaiting examination swore that they had lost many more dollars than the law required for entry, and the government simply took their word for it.

Just 300 yards away were several United States Navy ammunition boats loaded with powder. If the wind had been blowing in their direction, the tale told next morning might have been far more terrible.

A young couple from Saxony were forced to postpone their impending wedding and remain at the Barge Office until they could receive more money from home. Because the groom, a divorced man, had found legal difficulties in the way of his new marriage in Europe, the two had brought over from the old country a complete outfit for immediate housekeeping. When it was destroyed, they sat down woefully to wait for remuneration from their relatives in Saxony.

The New York World commented in blistering terms on the liability of the government for the disaster: "If a private individual or corporation had put up huge buildings of inflammable pine on a little island in the bay, and had kept there as many as 3,500 persons from all over the Earth, public opinion would have risen in its might. But the United States government did it."

On July 1, 1897, two weeks after the fire, President William McKinley went before Congress with a recommendation that $600,000 be appropriated to replace the destroyed structures with fireproof buildings. The present structures are the result of his recommendation.

On December 17, 1900, the new stone Main Building was opened and 2,251 immigrants were received that day. Meanwhile, Ellis Island was the storm center of the national immigration debate. In May 1909, so vituperative was the criticism of the island that John H. Clark of the Montreal Immigration Station declined the appointment as Commissioner at Ellis Island.

While the fire of 1897 may have been the worst disaster to occur on Ellis Island, it was not the only one. An explosion of dynamite took place at a pier on the New Jersey shore within a few hundred feet of the New York Central Railroad ferry house on the afternoon of February 1, 1911, shaking New York and New Jersey over a 40-mile radius, causing several thousand dollars worth of damage at Ellis Island, and by a strange quirk of fate narrowly missing the destruction of several hundred immigrants.

An unknown number of men near the dynamite, including members of the crew, were killed, and hundreds were injured. Thousands of windows were broken in lower Manhattan and Jersey City, while first examinations at Ellis Island indicated a property damage which could not be estimated.

At noon, men were transferring boxes of dynamite from the boat, *Whirtle*, to cars at the end of the pier. The Norwegian ship *Ingrid* was discharging a cargo of bone at the same time. Several lighters were moored nearby, and more than half of them were destroyed by the explosion.

According to the records, all lower Manhattan was in a turmoil, and the shock was felt as far north as Columbia University. The pier also contained a long train of cars, every one of which was damaged. About 200 buildings in lower Manhattan were rocked to the point of imperilling their occupants. No licenses had been issued for the moving of the dynamite, and seven officers of the New York Central and DuPont Powder Company — owners of the ship — were arrested.

Coming as it did, at noontime, the complete destruction of all the immigrants at Ellis Island was prevented. If the explosion had happened 30 minutes sooner or later, the chances are that all immigrants, who had just filed from the big detention room to the lunch room, would have been killed. Immigration was heavy in that year, and it is certain that there would have been many casualties.

It was a clear day, but with the first explosion, muddy rain water swept up from the

38

bay, stains from which never came off the clothing of those exposed to the deluge. The residue showered down upon the island, and all the hospital attendants and nurses in white uniforms were covered with the black smudge.

As the great ocean liners wearing the insignia of the White Star, Red Star, Cunard, and Hamburg-America lines arrived in New York Harbor, their first and second class passengers were not required to undergo the inspection process at Ellis Island. Instead, these passengers underwent a cursory inspection aboard ship, the theory being that if a person could afford to purchase a first or second class ticket, they were less likely to become a public charge in America due to medical or legal reasons.

The federal government felt that these more affluent passengers would not end up in institutions or hospitals, or become a burden to the state. However, first and second class passengers were sent to Ellis Island for further inspection if they were sick or had legal problems.

For the third class or "steerage" passengers, things were different. These immigrants traveled in crowded and often unsanitary conditions near the bottom of steamships with few amenities, often spending up to two weeks seasick in their bunks during rough Atlantic Ocean crossings. Upon arrival in New York City, ships would dock at the Hudson or East River piers. First and second class passengers would disembark, pass through Customs at the piers and were free to enter the United States, while the steerage and third class passengers were transported from the pier by ferry or barge to Ellis Island, where everyone among them would undergo a medical and legal inspection.

If the immigrants' papers were in order and they were in reasonably good health, the Ellis Island inspection process would last approximately three to five hours. The inspections took place in the Registry Room — known as the Great Hall — where doctors would briefly scan every immigrant for obvious physical ailments.

Doctors at Ellis Island soon became very adept at conducting these "six-second physicals." By 1916, it was said that a doctor could identify numerous medical conditions —

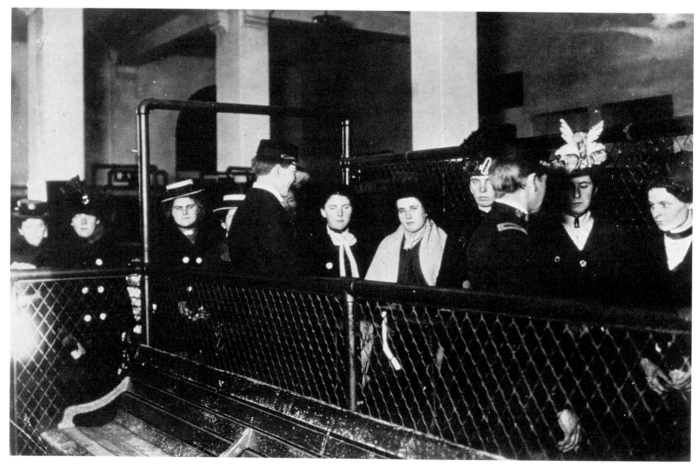

ranging from anemia to goiters to varicose veins — just by glancing at an immigrant. The ship's manifest log, which had been filled out back at the port of embarkation, contained the immigrant's name and his/her answers to 29 questions. This document was used by the legal inspectors at Ellis Island to cross-examine the immigrant during the legal (or primary) inspection.

The two agencies responsible for processing immigrants at Ellis Island were the United States Public Health Service and the United States Bureau of Immigration, the forerunner of today's Immigration and Naturalization Service.

Despite the island's reputation as an "Island of Tears," the vast majority of immigrants were treated courteously and respectfully, and were free to begin their new lives in America after only a few short hours on Ellis Island. Only two percent of the arriving immi-

grants were excluded from entry. The two main reasons why an immigrant would be excluded were if a doctor diagnosed that the immigrant had a contagious disease that would endanger the public health, or if a legal inspector thought the immigrant was likely to become a public charge or an illegal contract laborer.

Opposition to Immigration

The first vigorous reaction against immigration resulted from the wave of immigration in the middle of the nineteenth century. Unfortunately, this movement took the form of a strong religious opposition. The Irish were largely Roman Catholics. The American, or "Know-Nothing," Party nominated candidates in national elections and carried on an intensive campaign of propaganda. It sought the restriction of immigration and, especially, the exclusion of Roman Catholics. The crisis

Above: As seen in this 1922 photograph, medical inspections were part of the processing experienced by immigrants who arrived at Ellis Island. Most people were cleared for entry in less than five hours.

over slavery in the Civil War served to abate this movement, but only for the time being. Meanwhile, Irish-born Catholics enlisted and died by thousands for the sake of preserving the Union. On the Southern side, Father Grady became the beloved poet of the Confederate cause.

The opposition to immigration on religious grounds rose periodically. Before the Civil War, it was "Know-Nothingism." In the 1890s, it was the American Protective Association. In the 1920s, this nefarious cause was heralded by the notorious Ku Klux Klan. Historically important in the history of opposition to immigration is that which was voiced by labor unions and America's blue-collar working people over the issue of job competition.

Chinese Immigration

Immigration by the Chinese into the United States is often overlooked in general histories of immigration because it was largely confined to the Pacific Coast states and such immigration gateways as San Francisco, and hence, far from the important American cities such as New York. However, the immigration of the Chinese people into the United States had an essential impact upon the western part of the United States, not only in terms of ethnic composition, but in terms of American history. It was, after all, Chinese laborers who were responsible for the construction of the Central Pacific Railroad, the western portion of the first United States transcontinental railroad.

Before 1851, official records showed that only 46 Chinese had entered the United States, although a number of them had probably entered California before it became a state. In the decade of the 1850s, however, the United States would welcome 41,397 Chinese, with another 64,301 arriving in the 1860s.

Work was begun on the Central Pacific at Sacramento, California in January 1863. Over the next six years, thousands of Chinese workers came into California to help in the laying of the tracks and the other construction projects necessary to make the railroad a reality. The work done by the Chinese included the difficult crossing of the Sierra Nevada, which took place between 1864 and 1868, and which represented the greatest engineering feat to date in American railroad history. The following year, as Chinese crews were constructing the railroad across the Great Basin desert in Utah, they succeeded in laying

an unprecedented 10 miles of track in a single day.

While it may have been the railroad era that accounted for the most memorable moments in early Chinese-American history, the great California Gold Rush of 1849 was the true catalyst for the first major wave of Chinese immigration. As with the people of other nations, the population of the Chinese Empire was represented in the great rush for California which took place during the gold excitement.

At the beginning of 1849, there were only an estimated 54 Chinese people in California. At the news of the gold discovery, a steady immigration commenced which continued until 1876, at which time the Chinese in the United States numbered 151,000, of whom 116,000 were in the state of California.

This increase in their numbers, rapid even in comparison with the general increase in population, was largely due to the fact that before the completion of the transcontinental railroad in 1869, China was nearer to the shores of California than was the eastern portion of the United States.

Another circumstance which contributed to the heavy influx of Chinese into the United States was the fact that news of the gold discovery found southeastern China in poverty and ruin caused by the infamous Taiping Rebellion. Shipping companies made the most of this by distributing maps and pamphlets with highly colored accounts of the golden hills of California.

The adventurous and hard-working Chinese people came to work in the mines, but also found jobs as cooks, laundrymen, and laborers in other industries. Chinese workers, known in the contemporary vernacular as "coolies," were much in demand as laborers and carpenters, and many Chinese entrepreneurs soon started restaurants and laundries. The word itself comes from two Chinese words, "koo," which roughly translated meant

to rent, and "lee," which was interpreted as denoting strength. The coolies are those who rent out their strength, that is, they were unskilled laborers.

California's Governor McDougal referred to the Chinese as "among the most worthy of our newly adopted citizens." The Chinese went on to play a prominent part in the parades in celebration of the admission of

Above: A street scene in San Francisco, circa 1900.

Opposite: A Chinese woman in traditional costume.

Below and opposite bottom: San Francisco scenes, 1901.

Above: A Chinese immigrant woman with bound feet.

Below: A Chinese immigrant child in an embroidered jacket, circa 1900.

the state to the Union in 1850. They were everywhere welcomed and their wages were such that they could save a substantial part to send back to the families they had left at home in China.

The Chinese were welcomed as long as the surface gold was plentiful enough to make rich all who came. But that situation was not long to continue. By the mid to late 1850s, the major gold production was in deep mines requiring substantial investment by large companies. The days of the small entrepreneur gold prospector were over. The latter gold-seekers were disappointed. In the bitterness of their disappointment they turned upon the men of other races who were working side by side with them and accused them of stealing their wealth. They boldly asserted that California's gold belonged to them. The cry of "California for the Americans" was raised and taken up on all sides.

The French and Mexicans were driven out and the full force of anti-foreign persecution fell on the Chinese, who were, by their appearance, the most conspicuous body of immigrants. The state legislature was wholly in sympathy with the anti-foreign movement, and as early as 1850 passed the Foreign Miners' License law. This imposed a tax of 20 dollars a month on all foreign miners. Instead of bringing into the state treasury the revenue promised by its framers, this law had the effect of depopulating some camps and of seriously injuring all of them. San Francisco became overrun with penniless foreigners and their care became a serious problem. The law was conceded to be a failure and was repealed the following year. In 1858, the California legislature passed a law forbidding Chinese to land on the California coast except by stress of weather, but this law was declared unconstitutional by the Supreme Court.

The beginning of work on the Central Pacific Railroad found many Chinese employed on the construction work, despite general anti-Chinese sentiment in much of the West. The scarcity of labor caused the railroad construction supervisors to actively recruit Chinese immigrants. In order to get them to California, it was necessary to advance their passage-money and other expenses. To cover this loan each Chinese man employed signed a promissory note for $75. This note provided for monthly installment payments running over a period of seven months and was endorsed by friends in China. Each laborer was guaranteed a wage of $35 a month.

Ironically, it was in 1862, the first year of the building of the Central Pacific, that the United States Congress passed the first Chinese exclusion law. The official act passed by the United States Congress, and signed into law by President Abraham Lincoln on February 19, 1862, prohibited the transportation on American vessels of Chinese immigrant workers.

It was also in 1862 that a head tax was imposed by the California legislature on the Chinese, and, although it would be repealed, a year later the California legislature passed a law excluding Chinese from public schools.

During the Civil War other issues overshadowed the Chinese question and they had a brief respite. But in 1868 the Burlingame Treaty was entered into between the United States and China. It provided for reciprocal exemption from persecution on account of religious belief, the privilege of schools and colleges, and in fact it agreed that every Chinese citizen in the United States should have every privilege which was expected by the American citizens in China. Though naturalization was especially excepted, the provisions of this treaty aroused a storm of antagonism on the Pacific Coast. The labor agitators decried the treaty as a betrayal of the American working man, and the whole Chinese question was once again in more violent form, this time more than ever before.

In 1870, the California legislature passed a law imposing a fine of up to $5,000 for "bringing Chinese into State without a certificate of good character." This was soon declared unconstitutional by the United States Supreme Court.

United States nineteenth century legislative history as it relates to Chinese immigration had several curious ironies. In the 1870s, it seemed to be aimed at "protecting" Chinese immigrants from unscrupulous labor contractors, but by the 1880s, it was aimed simply at excluding Chinese immigration. During the period from 1861 to 1870, 64,301 Chinese people had immigrated into the United States as opposed to 41,397 in the previous decade.

Between 1871 and 1880, Chinese immigration doubled to 123,201, but during the 1880s restrictive legislation curbed it to 61,711, and in the 1890s, the total Chinese immigrants numbered just 14,799.

The official act passed by the United States Congress, and signed into law by President Ulysses S. Grant on March 3, 1875 established the policy of direct federal regulation of immigration by prohibiting for the first time entry to undesirable immigrants. The act of 1875 excluded criminals and prostitutes from admission to the United States, but it also prohibited the bringing of "any Oriental persons without their free and voluntary consent." The law also declared as a felony the contracting to supply the labor of the Chinese immigrant workers.

In 1879, the United States Congress passed a bill restricting Chinese immigration, but President Rutherford B. Hayes vetoed the bill. In 1880, however, a treaty was negotiated between the United States and China by which the United States was empowered to suspend immigration of laborers. It was ratified by the United States Senate on May 5, 1881. The following year, the United States Congress passed the Chinese Exclusion Act. Signed into law by President Chester Alan Arthur on May 6, 1882, the notorious Chinese Exclusion Act

officially suspended immigration of Chinese laborers to the United States for 10 years, provided for deportation of Chinese illegally in the United States, and barred Chinese from naturalization. However, the Chinese Exclusion Act did permit Chinese laborers already in the United States to remain in the country after a temporary absence, and it permitted the entry of Chinese students, teachers, merchants, or those "proceeding to the United States. . . from curiosity."

Above: Chinese immigrants in New York City's Chinatown, circa 1900.

Below: In the 1890s, publication of photos such as this one of an opium den helped to create anti-Chinese feelings.

Above: An immigrant's eye view of the Statue of Liberty in New York Harbor.

Below: A large steamship enters New York Harbor from the Atlantic. The Statue of Liberty is on the left, while Ellis Island can be seen immediately above the ship.

the city seated in an open car with Toy Kaye Lowe, president of the Chinese Improvement Association. On December 17, 1943, all the Chinese exclusion laws would be repealed by the United States Congress. Chinese immigration had reached its peak during the 1870s with 123,201 and had declined steadily after that. Even during the 1940s, only 16,709 Chinese immigrated into the United States, fewer than in any previous decade of the twentieth century except the Depression era of the 1930s. The peak years of the 1870s would not be surpassed until the 1970s, when 124,326 Chinese people immigrated. The total increased to 346,747 in the 1980s and continued to increase to a 1994 annual peak of 58,867.

The Statue of Liberty

While the immigration station on Ellis Island played its vital and important role in the actual process of immigration, the statue on Liberty Island — formerly Bedloe's Island — a few hundred yards away, had played an equally important *symbolic* role in the history of immigration into the United States. The story of the Statue of Liberty began when the French sculptor Frederic Auguste Bartholdi was commissioned to design a sculpture with the year 1876 in mind for completion, to commemorate the centennial of the American Declaration of Independence.

The Statue was a joint effort between America and France, and it was agreed upon that the American people were to build the pedestal, and the French people were responsible for the statue and its assembly in the United States. However, lack of funds was a problem on both sides of the Atlantic Ocean. In France, public fees, various forms of entertainment, and a lottery were among the methods used to raise funds. In the United States, benefit theatrical events, art exhibitions, auctions and prize fights assisted in providing needed funds. Meanwhile in France, Bartholdi required the assistance of an engineer to address structural issues associated with designing such as colossal copper sculpture.

Alexandre Gustave Eiffel — designer of the Eiffel Tower — was commissioned to design the massive iron pylon and secondary skeletal framework which allows the Statue's copper skin to move independently yet stand upright. Back in America, fund-raising for the pedestal was going particularly slowly, so

The official acts passed by the United States Congress, and signed into law by President Theodore Roosevelt on April 29, 1902 and on April 27, 1904, extended the existing Chinese exclusion acts until "such time as a new treaty with China was negotiated, and extend the application of the exclusion acts to insular territories of the United States, including the requirement of a certificate of residence, except in Hawaii."

Within a few years, however, there would be a complete change of attitude in California toward the Chinese. Harassment ceased and Chinese soon became prosperous citizens. The native-born Chinese became registered voters. In 1927, when James Rolph was reelected as mayor of San Francisco, he toured

Joseph Pulitzer (noted for the Pulitzer Prize) opened up the editorial pages of his newspaper, *The World*, to support the fund-raising effort. Pulitzer used his newspaper to criticize both the rich who had failed to finance the pedestal construction and the middle class who were content to rely upon the wealthy to provide the funds. Pulitzer's campaign of harsh criticism was successful in motivating the people of America to donate.

Financing for the pedestal was completed in August 1885, and pedestal construction was finished in April of 1886. The Statue was completed in France in July, 1884 and arrived in New York Harbor in June of 1885 on board the French frigate *Isere* which transported the Statue of Liberty from France to the United States. In transit, the Statue was reduced to 350 individual pieces and packed in 214 crates. The Statue was reassembled on the pedestal in four months' time. On October 28, 1886, the dedication of the Statue of Liberty took place in front of thousands of spectators. She was a centennial gift 10 years late.

The story of the statue and her island has been one of change. The statue was placed upon her new pedestal on Bedloe's Island inside the courtyard of the star-shaped walls of Fort Wood, which had been completed for the War of 1812. The United States Lighthouse Board had responsibility for the operation of the Statue of Liberty until 1901. After 1901, the care and operation of the Statue was placed under the jurisdiction of the United States War Department.

A Presidential Proclamation declared Fort Wood, and the Statue of Liberty within it, a National Monument on October 15th, 1924, and the monument's boundary was set at the outer edge of Fort Wood. In 1933, the care and administration of the National Monument was transferred to the National Park Service. On September 8, 1937, jurisdiction was enlarged to encompass all of Bedloe's Island and in 1956, the island's name was changed to Liberty Island. On May 11, 1965, Ellis Island was transferred to the National Park Service and became part of the Statue of Liberty National Monument

The height from base to torch is 151 feet, one inch. From the ground to the tip of the torch is 305 feet, one inch and from the heel to the top of the head is 111 feet, one inch. Today, visitors climb 354 steps to reach

the crown, or 192 steps in order to reach the top of the pedestal. There are 25 windows in the crown which symbolize 25 gemstones found on the Earth. The seven rays of the Statue's crown represent the seven seas and the seven continents of the world. The tablet which the Statue holds in her left hand reads — in Roman numerals — "July 4th, 1776." The total weight of copper in the Statue is 62,000 pounds and the total weight of steel in the Statue is 250,000 pounds. The total weight of the Statue's concrete foundation is 54 million pounds. The cooper sheeting of the Statue is 3/32 of an inch thick or 2.37mm.

Above: The main docking area on Liberty Island, formerly Bedloe's Island, as seen in about 1900.

Below: A view of Governor's Island in New York Harbor. The Statue of Liberty can be seen in the distance.

THE EARLY
TWENTIETH CENTURY

After the enormous wave of immigrants that had come into the United States during the last quarter of the nineteenth century, it was widely believed the numbers would fall in the twentieth century, but that was not the case. In fact, the number of immigrants would increase dramatically: indeed, 1907 would mark the year in which more people would enter the United States as immigrants than any other in history.

The Great Wave of Immigration

Between the years of 1901 and 1910, a total of 8,795,386 immigrants entered the United States, more than any other decade in history. Four years, 1905, 1906, 1907, and 1910, would top a million, an occurrence that has never again been repeated. The peak year of the decade came in 1907, with a total of 1,285,349 immigrants. It was a record that would be topped only by the 1,536,483 who entered in 1990, and the 1,877,167 people who entered in 1991. The largest nationality group among the 8,795,386 of 1901-1910 were the 2,145,266 who arrived from the Austro-Hungarian Empire, closely followed by 2,045,877 who arrived from Italy.

There were 1,597,306 who arrived from Russia, and 865,015 who immigrated from the United Kingdom, including 339,065 people from Ireland. Many of those coming from the imploding Austrian and Russian Empires were Jews who were coming to escape the tyranny of the Old World for the freedom and promise of the New World, a place where determination and hard work would reap rewards not possible under the emperors.

By the beginning of the twentieth century many flaws appeared in the naturalization system begun by Congress in 1790. These problems were largely due to a complete lack of uniformity in the practices of naturalization courts. No single system set standards for proof of eligibility, proof of new citizenship, or record keeping. For example, many courts routinely naturalized large groups of people on the eve of political elections, often without asking if they met the legal conditions. Because fraud became prevalent, respect for the naturalization process declined.

In February 1903, when Congress approved the transfer of immigration work from the Secretary of the Treasury to the Secretary of a newly created Department of Commerce and Labor, the Office of Immigration became the Bureau of Immigration. The official act passed by the United States Congress, and signed into law by President Theodore Roosevelt on February 14, 1903, expanded the authority of the commissioner general of Immigration in the areas of rule-making and enforcement of immi-

Below: A nervous family undergoes line inspection at Ellis Island in 1910.

Opposite: A proud young immigrant boy, about to become an American.

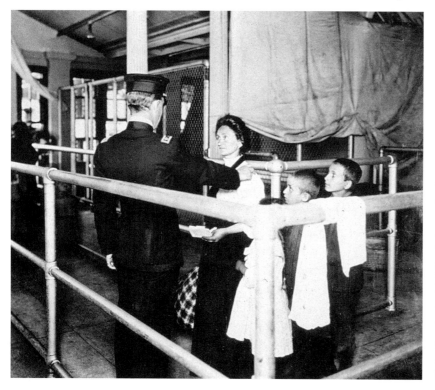

gration laws. Signed by President Roosevelt two weeks later, on March 3, the Immigration Act of 1903 was to be an extensive codification of existing immigration law.

In 1905 a special commission investigated and reported on the flaws in the naturalization process. Based on that report, Congress passed the Naturalization Act of 1906, which framed the basic rules for naturalization still in effect today. Also, because the law made granting citizenship a federal responsibility, Congress increased the Bureau of Immigration's functions and renamed it the Bureau of Immigration and Naturalization.

This federal agency now supervised naturalization, though the courts retained the power to grant or deny citizenship. The 1906 act assigned naturalization forms, and required filing duplicates of every naturalization paper and fee with the bureau. Finally, applicants had

to speak English and sign their petition in their handwriting. To safeguard against possible fraud, guidelines provided for the cancellation of certificates.

The Immigration Act of 1903 was in direct response to a growing fear of international anarchy. It added to the list of inadmissible immigrants by being the first measure to provide for the exclusion of aliens on the grounds of proscribed opinions by excluding anarchists, or persons who believed in or advocated the overthrow by force or violence the government of the United States — or of all government, or of all forms of law — or the assassination of public officials.

The act also extended the period during which an alien who was inadmissible at the time of entry could be deported to three years after entry. It provided for the deportation of aliens who became public charges within two years after entry from causes existing prior to their landing. The Immigration Act of 1903 reaffirmed the Contract Labor Law of 1885.

The naturalization aspect of immigration policy did not come into being until the Naturalization Act of 1906, passed by Congress and signed by President Roosevelt on June 29. It combined the immigration and naturalization functions of the federal government. It also made knowledge of the English language a requirement for naturalization. Before then, naturalization was a function of the courts. The new law created the Bureau of Immigration and Naturalization, a forerunner of today's Immigration and Naturalization Service, and made it responsible for administering and enforcing United States immigration laws and for supervising the naturalization of aliens and keeping naturalization records.

This combined function lasted only seven years, however, and naturalization became a separate bureau again in 1913, when the Department of Commerce and Labor was split into two departments. Both functions moved to the new Department of Labor, which left the commissioner general in charge of the Bureau of Immigration and named a new Commissioner for the Bureau of Naturalization. They remained separate until

1933, when they were consolidated by Executive Order to form the Immigration and Naturalization Service, still within the Labor Department.

The Bureau of Immigration and Naturalization established various fundamental procedural safeguards regarding naturalization, such as fixed fees and uniform naturalization forms.

The Immigration Act of 1907, passed by Congress and signed by President Roosevelt on February 20, is seen in legislative history as the first major codifying act since 1903 to consolidate earlier legislation. It required aliens to declare "intention of permanent or temporary stay in the United States," and officially classified arriving aliens as "immigrants" or "nonimmigrants." It should be pointed out that it was not until the sweeping Immigration Act of 1924 that the term "nonimmigrant" would be officially defined as "all other alien entries into the United States."

The Immigration Act of 1907 reaffirmed the requirement for manifesting of aliens arriving by water and added a like requirement with regard to departing aliens.

The new codification also added various groups to the list of "excludable classes." Specifically, these were imbeciles, feeble-minded persons, persons with physical or mental defects which may affect their ability to earn a living, persons afflicted with tuberculosis, children unaccompanied by their parents, persons who admitted the commission of a crime involving moral turpitude, and women coming to the United States for immoral purposes. Exempted from the provisions of the Contract Labor Law were professional actors, artists, singers, ministers, professors, and domestic servants.

The Immigration Act of 1907 extended the authority to deport any alien who had become a public charge from causes which existed prior to that alien's entry from two to three years. In a controversial provision that was seen as being aimed at Japanese laborers, it also authorized the President to refuse admission to certain persons when he or she was satisfied that their immigration was seen as detrimental to labor conditions within the United States.

There was a long and curious list of the epithets hurled at the immigrant during this

Above: A young immigrant mill worker, circa 1908.

Overleaf: A map of the Austro-Hungarian Empire, circa 1900, showing the regions from which 2,145,266 people immigrated during the first decade of the twentieth century.

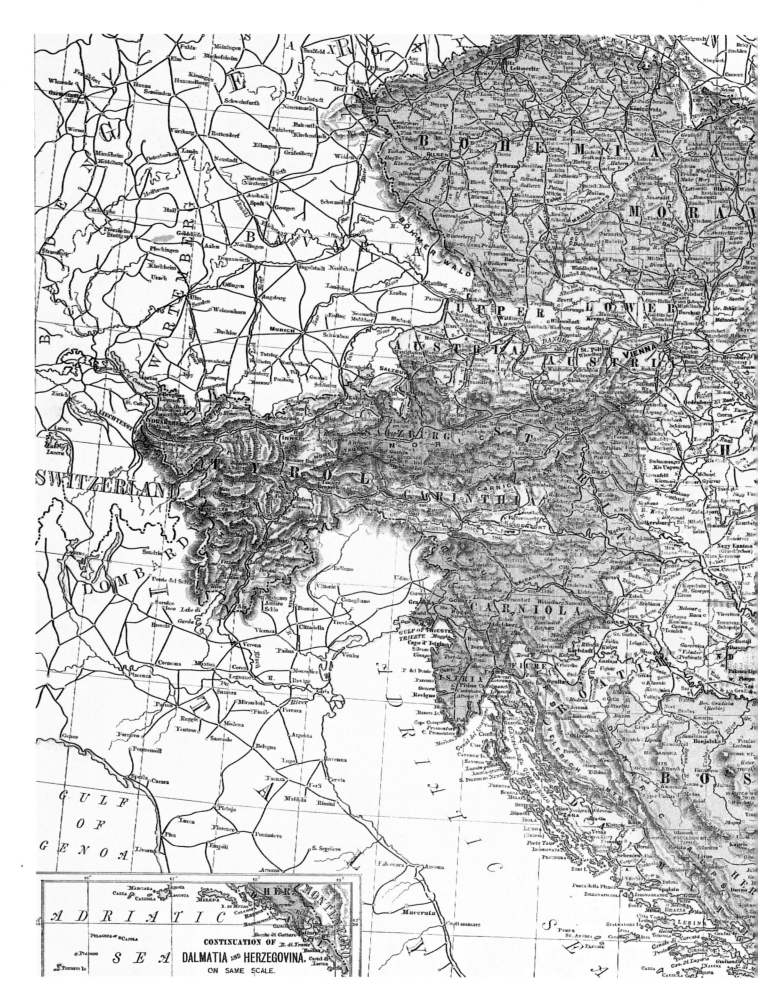

CONTINUATION OF
DALMATIA AND HERZEGOVINA,
ON SAME SCALE.

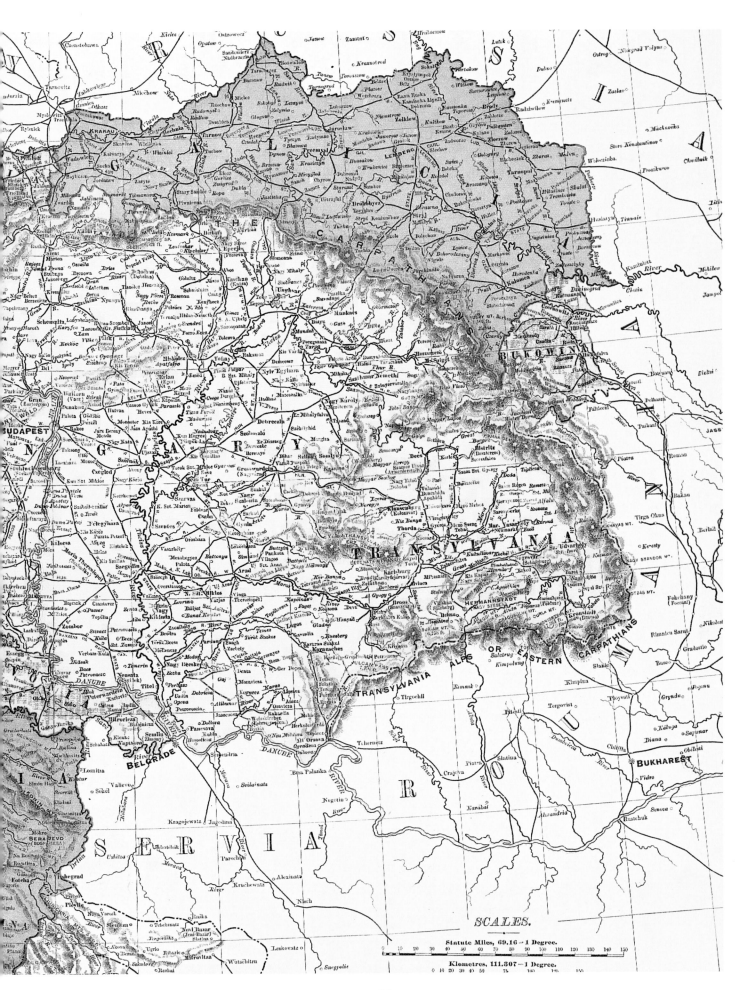

SCALES.

Statute Miles, 69.16 = 1 Degree.

Kilometres, 111.307 = 1 Degree.

Below: Italian immigrants being processed at Ellis Island in 1912. During the second decade of the twentieth century, over two million Italians arrived in the United States, more than in any other decade in history.

period. The immigrants were derided as "lawless, immoral, vicious, criminal." They were called "social dregs and rogues, vicious off-scourings."

The history of the anti-immigration movement has some curious moments. The United States has seen the foreign-born themselves engaged in opposition to bringing in more workers when there was no employment, just as the owners of big business that used to be called the "captains of industry" were desperately fighting against restrictive legislation. On November 22, 1908, Ignace Paderewski, the noted Polish-born pianist, declared that constant foreign immigration to the United States was threatening the strength and character of the American people. Coming from a Pole, this was a curious statement.

In May 1908, Professor Lotoslavski of Moscow University had predicted that America would have "political indigestion" if it attempted to assimilate its foreign population. United States Secretary of State Elihu Root caused much agitation that same year by declaring that foreign immigration had created conditions in the United States similar to those in Rome, when Rome was overrun by barbarians. On the same day, and coming as a curious coincidence, the liberal minister, Reverend F.H. Wright said, "Fusion of foreign blood is valuable, especially in preventing national degeneration."

In 1914, a curious book, *The Passing of the Great Race*, was published, in which author Madison Grant stated that "the Nordic race alone had created and fostered all the values of western civilization." The ancient Greeks, he held, were "Nordics" because they were brave. This extraordinary book closed by explaining that World War I was an effort on the part of the enemies of Germany to destroy the stronghold of Nordicism.

The rise in immigration in the early twentieth century occurred during a period of economic distress in the United States, and resulted in public demands for strict limits on immigration. When more than 1.2 million people migrated to the United States in 1907, a federal commission led by Senator William P. Dillingham began to study the problem. The commission's final report of 1911, known as the "Dillingham Report," filled 42 volumes and concluded that "The nation must regulate the kind or type of immigrants admitted."

Dillingham Commission recommendations influenced the Immigration Act of 1917, which restated all past exclusions and added two more. The first was a literacy requirement for all people entering the United States as immigrants. Second was exclusion of persons coming from a geographic area termed the "Asiatic Barred Zone" containing most of Asia and the Pacific Islands. The act also defined and expanded the powers of immigration officers, improved deportation practices, and created a system to admit certain excluded groups in special cases. The 1917 law also increased the head tax to $8.00 Since 1894, movements to limit or reduce immigration usually advocated raising the tax.

President Woodrow Wilson opposed any literacy test and vetoed the bill. Congress nevertheless mustered the majority needed to override the veto, and the bill passed on February 5, 1917. While this law regulated the selection of immigrants, there was still no attempt to limit the number of people admitted.

The Immigration Act of February 5, 1917 is significant in that it codified all previously enacted exclusion provisions. In addition, it excluded illiterate aliens from entry, it expanded the list of aliens excluded for mental health and other reasons, and it considerably broadened the classes of aliens deportable from the United States and introduced the requirement of deportation without statute of limitation in certain more serious cases.

The 1917 law further restricted the immigration of Asian persons, creating the barred zone which would be known as "The Asia-Pacific Triangle." The natives of this vast sector of the globe were declared inadmissible.

Meanwhile, the laws against contract labor had been hard to enforce. What, indeed, constituted a contract? The big American employers merely turned over the job of persuading the confiding immigrants to the shipping companies. The propaganda continued and opposition to immigration grew. From 1885 to 1917, the battle for the literacy test raged throughout the United States. During this generation, propaganda for the literacy test led both houses of Congress to take no less than 32 votes. Finally, in February 1917, just two months before the United States declared war on Germany and entered World War I, the literacy test law was passed over President Wilson's veto. Twice the president had hurled this bill back to Congress, but public sentiment at last forced its passage.

Between the years of 1911 and 1920, a total of 5,735,811 immigrants entered the United States. Of these, 2,416,372 arrived in 1913 and 1914 on the eve of World War I, while fewer than a million arrived between 1915 and 1919. Perhaps because of the fear of World War I and the demise of the Austro-Hungarian and Russian Empires, it was the second largest decade of immigration that the

United States had yet experienced, eclipsing even the 1880s. The largest nationality group to arrive between 1911 and 1920 were the 1,109,524 who arrived from Italy, followed by 921,201 people who fled the Russian Revolution, 896,342 who fled the collapse of the Austro-Hungarian Empire, and 742,185 who immigrated from Canada.

The Aftermath of World War I

The United States entry into World War I brought the country to the forefront of the stage of global politics. With a state of war came the realization that certain nations — such as Germany, Turkey, and Austria-Hungary — had the defeat of the United States as their national policy. There was also the nearly-successful ploy by the German foreign minis-

Above: Louis Hine's famous 1909 portrait of a young daughter of immigrants in Pittsburgh, Pennsylvania.

Overleaf: A map of the German Empire as it existed before World War I, showing the regions from which 167,517 people immigrated during the first decade of the twentieth century. During the two decades before, 1,958,122 people immigrated from the German states.

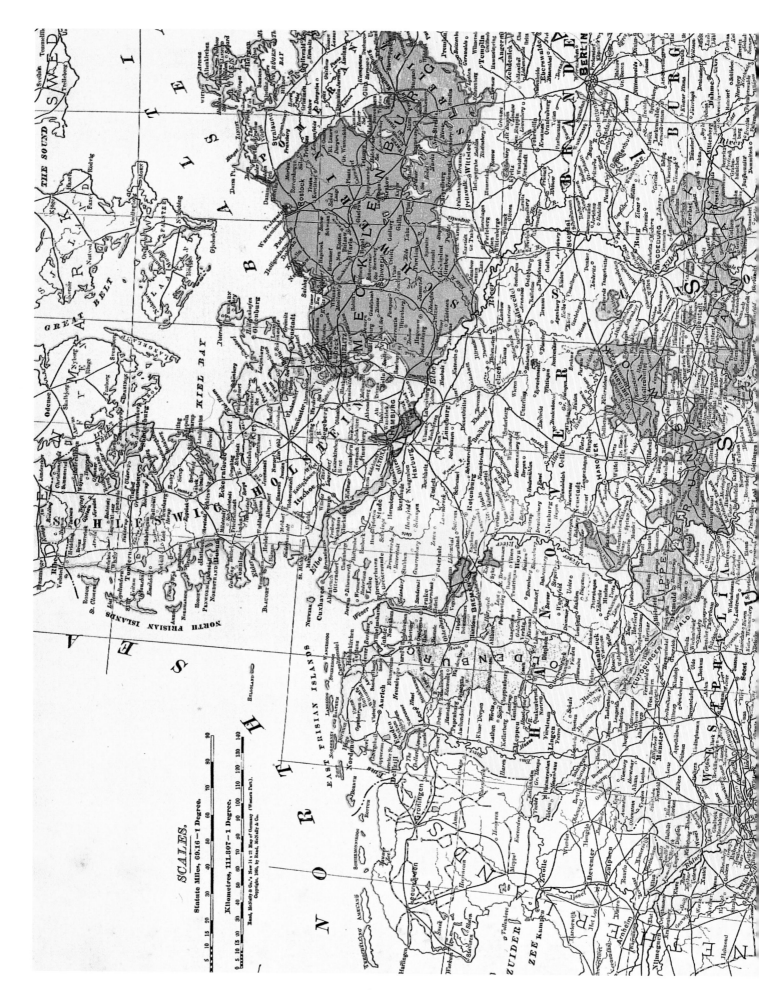

SCALES.

Statute Miles, 69.16=1 Degree.

Kilometres, 111.807=1 Degree.

Rand, McNally & Co.'s New 14 x 21 Map of Germany (Western Part).
Copyright, 1890, by Rand, McNally & Co.

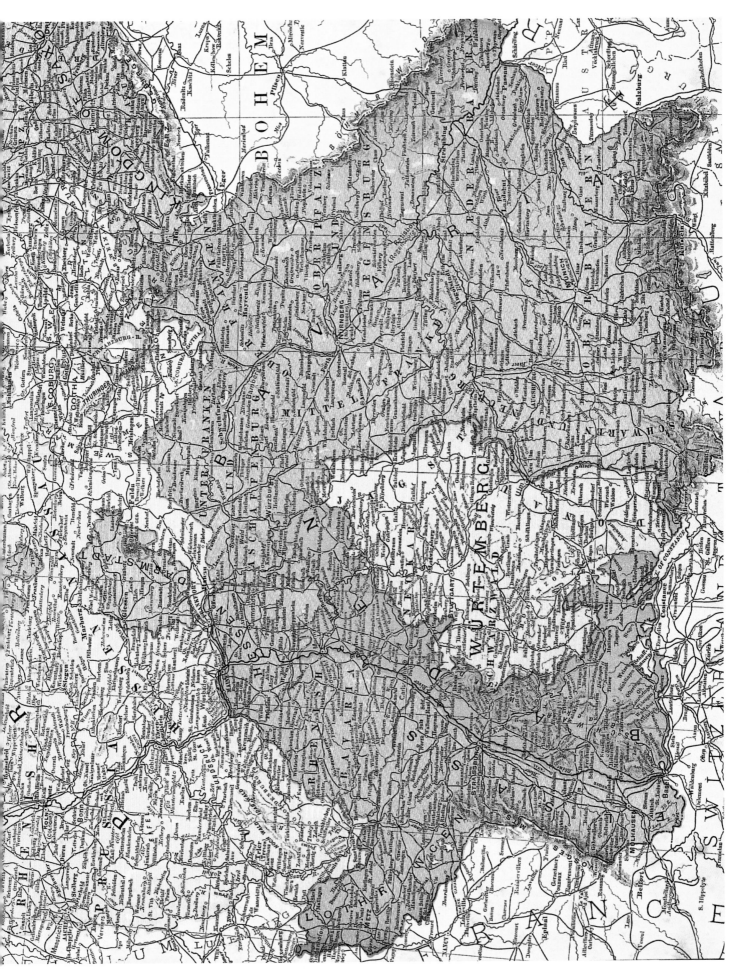

ter to draw Mexico into a declaration of war against the United States in order to take pressure off Germany.

The presence of enemy agents within the United States — including those involved in the Zimmerman plot — reinforced a desire to enlist the Bureau of Immigration in the protection of the United States. The Entry and Departure Controls Act passed by the United States Congress, and signed into law by President Woodrow Wilson on May 22, 1918, authorized the President — through the Bureau of Immigration — to control the departure and entry in times of war or national emergency of any alien whose presence was deemed contrary to public safety.

After the devastation of Europe by World War I, the volume of immigrants soared again. During 1920, the number of entries grew to three times that of 1919. At the same time, American unemployment and housing shortages grew. Many citizens either resented the flood of foreign workers with whom they competed for jobs, or feared foreign political ideas that they thought threatened American stability.

From this time on Americans' attitude toward immigration changed. Historically, they had regarded free and open immigration as healthy for the nation. As economic growth slowed and Americans experienced their first "Red Scare," opinion grew favoring laws to limit immigration even more strongly than the 1917 act did.

Within a few years of the Armistice, the fears of wartime emergency faded, and thoughts regarding immigration legislation returned to familiar themes. Numerous laws had been passed through the years to limit and/or control immigration, but, amazingly, it was not until 1921 that specific numbers were applied to this effort. Passed by the United States Congress and signed into law by the dynamic President Warren Gamaliel Harding on May 19, the Quota Law of 1921 was the first quantitative United States immigration law.

The Quota Law limited the number of aliens of any nationality entering the United States to three percent of the foreign-born persons of that nationality who had lived in the United States in 1910. Under the law signed by President Harding, approximately 350,000 such aliens were permitted to enter each year as quota immigrants, mostly from northern and western Europe. Exempted from this limitation were aliens who had resided continuously for at

least one year immediately preceding their application in one of the independent countries of the Western Hemisphere, nonimmigrant aliens such as government officials and their households, aliens in transit through the United States, temporary visitors for business and pleasure, and aliens whose immigration was regulated by immigration treaty.

As had been the case with previous immigration limitation legislation passed by the United States Congress, actors, artists, lecturers, singers, nurses, ministers, professors, domestic servants, and "aliens belonging to any recognized learned profession" were exempted and placed on a nonquota basis.

Two years later, the Quota Law was extended for two years — with amendments. In an official act passed by the United States Congress, and signed into law by President Harding on May 11, 1922, the residency requirement for immigrants from a Western Hemisphere country was changed from one year to five years. The 1922 law also "got tough" and authorized fines to be levied against transportation companies for "transporting an inadmissible alien unless it was deemed that inadmissibility was not known to the company

and could not have been discovered with reasonable diligence."

During the years of World War I, immigration dwindled to inconsequential proportions, but with the end of hostilities in Europe, and the imminent passage of the Act of 1921, the cavalcade from overseas once again swelled to record proportions. The final week before the new law became effective saw a mad dash of thousands to American shores. Ships carrying their human cargo raced into New York Harbor, actually colliding with one another in their hurry to be at Ellis Island before the last minute of grace. The *Saxonia* of the Cunard Line was one of the last of the immigrant ships to get under the wire, but there was no more room at Ellis Island. Guarded by United States Customs officials and Cunard Line detectives, her 800 passengers were landed on Pier 53 at the foot of West Thirteenth Street, where they camped for four days. Neither camp beds nor cots were available, but mattresses were supplied, and it was reported that these last-minute newcomers were well fed and comfortable.

While the immigrants, many of whom were Irish, were camped on the pier, some

Above: A group of Russian immigrants at Ellis Island in July 1923. By this time, the former Russian Empire was in a state of chaos following the Bolshevik takeover.

Overleaf: A map of Italy, circa 1900, showing the regions from which 2,045,877 people immigrated during the first decade of the twentieth century.

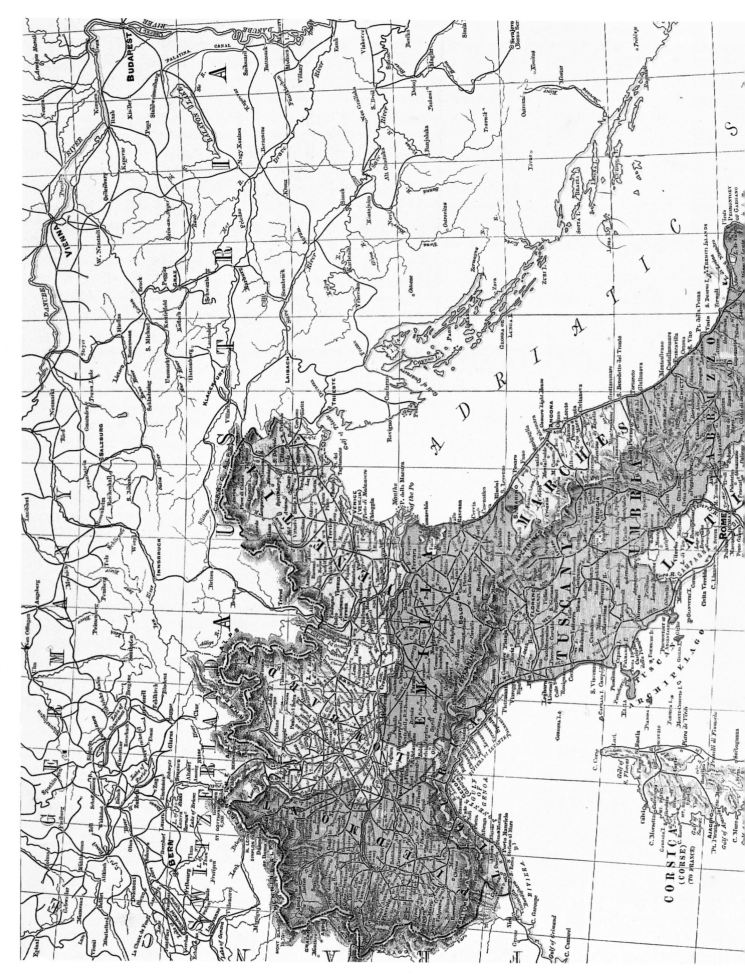

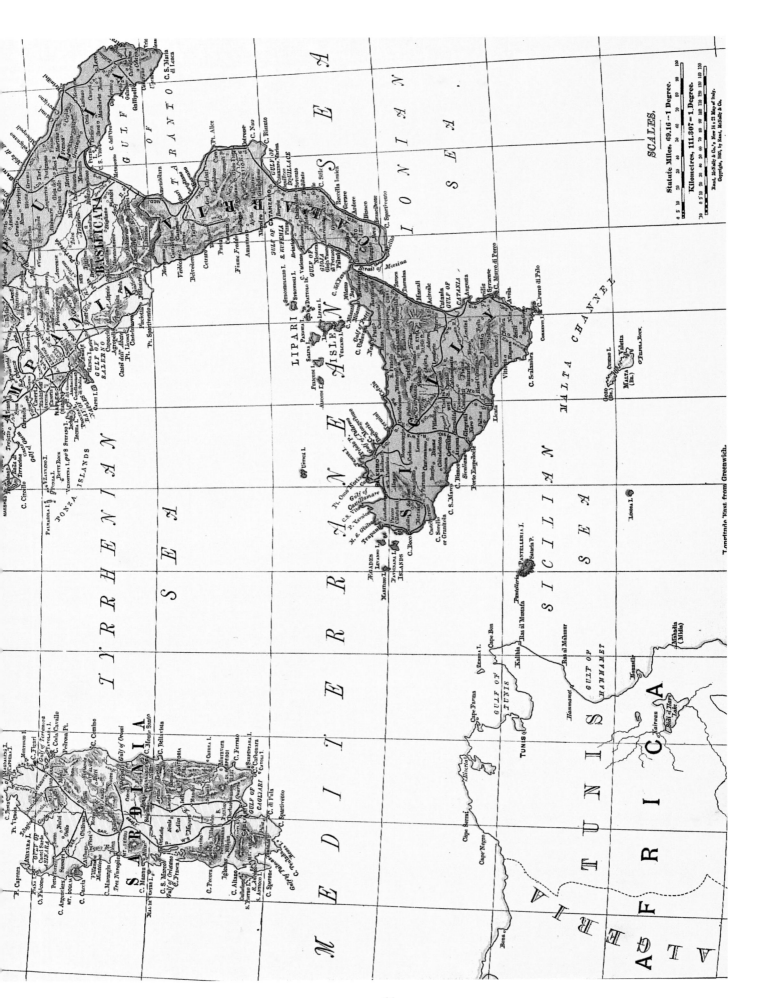

Below: European immigrant kiln workers in St. Louis, Missouri, circa 1904.

waved handkerchiefs from the windows to a group of their former fellow countrymen who were working at the Gansevoort Market. The workmen yelled, "Throw us a line, we'll give you some fruit." This was done and the Irish immigrants received enough bananas to supply every alien on the pier.

However, there was a storm of protest against the detention of incoming aliens in such an unbecoming manner. This criticism was further accentuated when customs officials assured the press that a squad of immigration inspectors and two physicians could have passed two-thirds of the persons held on the pier in less than five hours.

At the same time, the renewed rush to America revived all the canny wiles of the swindler. There is an account of a banker who was arrested for swindling 50 Russian immigrants out of an aggregate of $168,000. He loaned cash on jewels and other valuables to immigrants who wanted a start in business. When he had garnered most of the possessions of the Russians he left the country, but was apprehended on a ship at sea. Another banker was convicted of taking large sums of money

from immigrants for the supposed purpose of bringing their relatives to America. Of course the relatives never arrived. After several months this banker also disappeared but was finally caught and convicted.

In Cherbourg, France, in November 1920, 250 immigrants were left on the pier because they had bought worthless tickets.

During 1922 and 1923 the British were seriously concerned about cruelties and insults their countrymen were said to be suffering at Ellis Island. The United States immigrant station got a thorough trouncing in the House of Commons. Viscount Curzon, the Foreign Secretary, rose and stated that he knew personally of two English women who had been mistreated on Ellis Island and fed only bread and water. The British press wrote long articles about the inhumanity of keeping English citizens "in cages with people of dirtier and inferior nationalities."

While the Quota Law of 1921 had been the first immigration law passed by the United States Congress to use actual numeric quantification, the Immigration Act of 1924 was the first permanent limitation on immigration. Passed by Congress and signed into law by President Calvin Coolidge on May 26, the Immigration Act of 1924 established the National Origins Quota System.

Congress passed the 1924 law by a majority of 308 to 58 in the House of Representatives and 69 to nine in the Senate. It became a law with President Coolidge's signature on July 1, 1924.

Under the quota legislation of 1924, immigration was based on the numbers of the various national groups present in the United States population according to the census of 1890. The law originally permitted 15,000 to enter annually, and the proportions were made up according to the 1890 population percentages. Within just one decade, extra allowances would bring the total up to 164,667 in 1934. Of this total, Britain was allowed — together with Northern Ireland — a total of 65,721. Ireland (known as the Irish Free State until 1949) was permitted 17,853, and Germany, 25,957. Meanwhile Italy's quota was 5,802, and that of the Soviet Union was 2,712.

The second quota provision, which was to become permanent on July 1, 1927 — although it was later post-

Below: European immigrant kiln workers in St. Louis, Missouri, circa 1904.

poned to July 1, 1929 — would use the National Origins Quota System to set the annual quota for any country or nationality so that it would have "the same relation to 150,000 as the number of inhabitants in the continental United States in 1920 having that national origin had to the total number of inhabitants in the continental United States in 1920."

A Preference Quota Status was established for unmarried children under 21, for parents, for spouses of United States citizens over the age of 21, and for quota immigrants over 21 who were "skilled in agriculture" (together with their wives and dependent children under age 16). Nonquota status was accorded to wives and unmarried children under 18 of United States citizens, natives of Western Hemisphere countries and their families, nonimmigrants and certain others. Subsequent amendments would eliminate certain elements of this law's inherent discrimination against women, but comprehensive elimination was not achieved until 1952.

The Immigration Act of 1924 established the consular control system of immigration by mandating that "No alien may be permitted entrance to the United States without an unexpired immigration visa issued by an American consular officer abroad." Through this provision, the Bureau of Immigration — and later, its successor, the Immigration and Naturalization Service — would share control of immigration with the United States Department of State.

Among the other provisions of the sweeping Immigration Act of 1924 mandate was the introduction of a rule that no alien ineligible to become a citizen would be admitted to the United States as an immigrant. In retrospect, this provision is seen as having been directed primarily at Japanese aliens. The 1924 Act also imposed fines on transportation companies who landed aliens in violation of United States immigration laws. Since the 1924 law required immigrants to obtain visas in advance from United States embassies in their countries of origin, health inspections would be conducted there as well. By 1917, the Immigration Bureau sent officers to various foreign cities to advise the consuls there. The Public Health Service performed medical examinations of immigrants at the point of departure. This saved much time for people passing

through American ports, and reduced the number of people who had to be excluded and sent back home. Meanwhile, transportation companies usually tried to confirm that all passengers would be admitted upon arrival in the United States. Beginning in 1903, ships' surgeons had been examining immigrants sailing to America to be sure they carried no "loathsome or dangerous contagious disease." Such diseases were grounds for exclusion since 1891, based on the immigration law's responsibility to protect the public health. In those years Americans worried most about cholera, trachoma, tuberculosis, and other such illnesses that were common at the time.

Late in the 1920s, there was a pair of immigration laws enacted in clarification of the Immigration Act of 1924. The first of these was the March 31, 1928 act that provided more time to work out computation of the quotas established by the Immigration Act of 1924 by postponing introduction of the quotas until July 1, 1929. The second, passed by the United States Congress, and signed into law by President Coolidge on April 2, 1928, provided that the Immigration Act of 1924 was not to be construed to limit the right of American Indians to cross the border, but with the proviso that the

Above: European immigrant workers at an ore-unloading facility in Cleveland, Ohio, circa 1906.

Overleaf: A map of Ireland as it appeared before 1921, when the British government granted independence to 26 of Ireland's 32 counties. During the first two decades of the twentieth century, 727,481 immigrants came to the United States from this embattled isle.

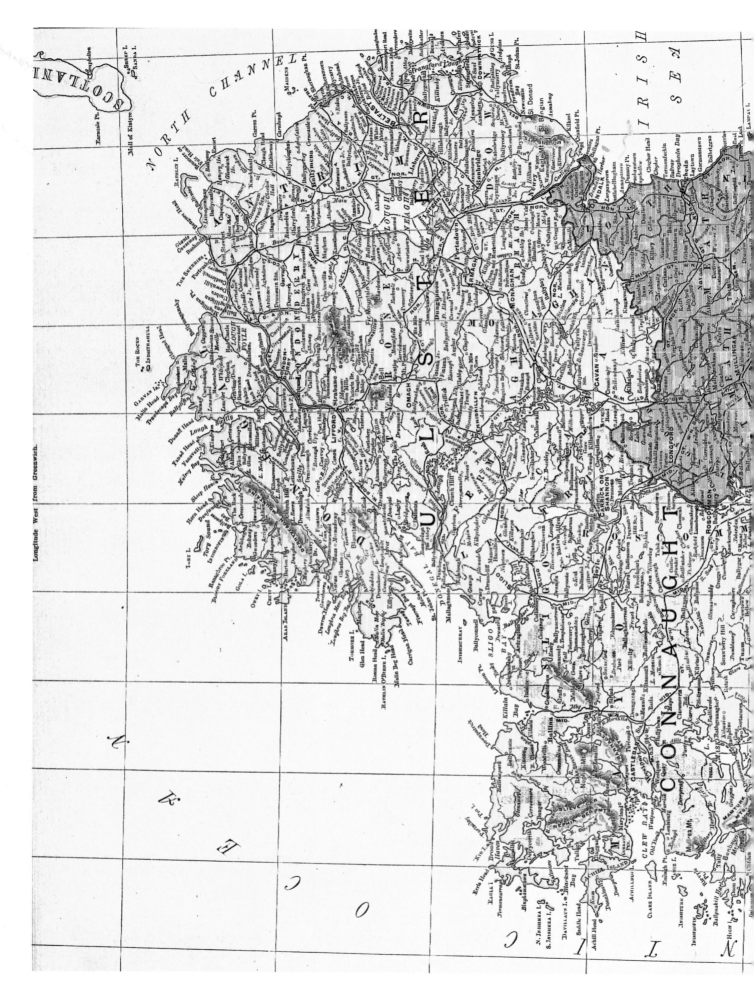

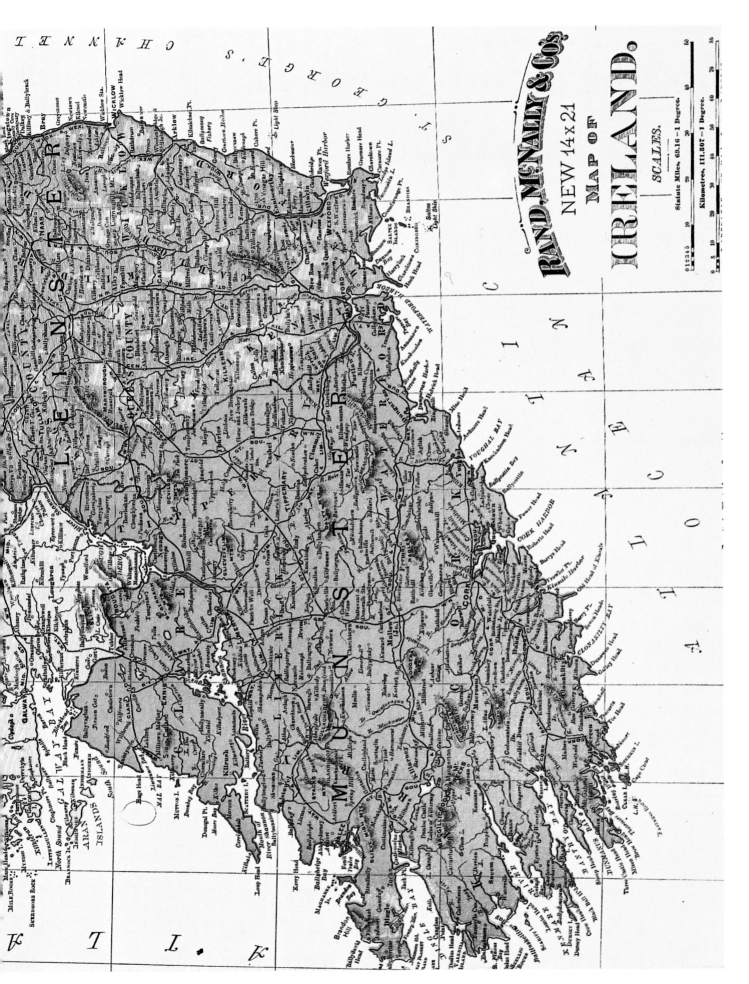

RAND, McNALLY & CO.'S
NEW 14 x 21
MAP OF
IRELAND.

SCALES.

Statute Miles, 69.16 = 1 Degree.

Kilometres, 111,307 = 1 Degree.

Above: President Coolidge signed the Immigration Act of 1924.

Below: A European immigrant worker in Chicago.

right did not extend to members of Indian tribes by adoption. In conjunction with the Immigration Act of 1917, the National Origins Quota System established by the Immigration Act of 1924 (and subsequent modifying or amending legislation) governed American immigration policy until 1952, when the provisions of the 1917-1929 legislation were superseded by the subsequent milestone Immigration and Nationality Act of 1952.

After the Immigration Act of 1924

Elected as vice president to Warren Gamaliel Harding in 1920, Vermont native Calvin Coolidge took office upon Harding's mysterious death in 1923 and won the White House in his own right in August 1924. Coolidge is of interest to historians of immigration for the fact that he signed more immigration legislation than any president before him, including the milestone Immigration Act of 1924 and all of its important amending legislation.

Coolidge is, despite his obvious interest in immigration policy, remembered for keeping a deliberately low presidential profile and for favoring minimal government intervention in the private sector. The son of a owner of a shop, he is known for his comment as President that "The business of America is business." The Registry Act of 1929 was signed by President Coolidge on March 2, 1929 as one of his last official acts. It amended existing immigration law by authorizing the establishment of a record of lawful admission for "certain aliens not ineligible for citizenship" when no record of admission for permanent residence could be found, and when the alien could prove that he or she entered the United States before July 1, 1924. This date was eventually pushed back to June 3, 1921 by the Act of August 7, 1939, which was, in turn, incorporated into the Alien Registration Act of 1940.

Two days later, on March 4, Coolidge signed another act which added two additional deportable classes to the Immigration Code defined by the 1917 and 1924 laws. These deportable classes were aliens convicted of carrying any weapon or bomb and sentenced to any term of six months or more, and aliens convicted of violation of the Prohibition law for which a sentence of one year or more was received. The March 4 law made reentry of a previously deported alien a felony punishable by fine or imprisonment or both. It also made entry by an alien at other than a designated place or by fraud to be a misdemeanor punishable by fine or imprisonment or both, and it deferred the deportation of an alien sentenced to imprisonment until the termination of the imprisonment.

Between the years of 1921 and 1930, a total of 4,107,209 immigrants entered the United States, fewer than during the two preceding decades because of the more restrictive immigration laws. The two largest nationality groups among the immigrants were both from the Western Hemisphere. These included 924,515 Canadians and 459,287 Mexicans.

Among European immigrants were 455,315 who arrived from Italy, followed by 412,202 who arrived from war-ravished Germany, where the economic distress gripping the Weimar Republic presaged the horrors of the impending Great Depression. The United Kingdom total was 339,570, which did not include the 211,234 who immigrated from Ireland, which became free of United Kingdom control in 1922.

Ellis Island Operations in the Early Twentieth Century

During the first decade of the twentieth century, United States immigration officials and planners mistakenly thought that the peak wave of immigration had already passed. Actually, immigration was on the rise. In 1907, more people immigrated to the United States than any other year. Just as legislation that would be passed between 1907 and 1917 took this into account, so too did the practical planning of facilities, especially those at America's doorstep — Ellis Island.

After nearly a century of state and local control of immigration, President Benjamin Harrison had ordered the construction of the federally-operated immigration station on Ellis Island. The facility had opened in 1892, and it was rebuilt to reopen in 1900 after being destroyed by fire in 1897. As immigration increased, masons and carpenters were constantly struggling to enlarge and build new facilities to accommodate this greater than anticipated influx of new immigrants. In the peak year of 1907 alone, approximately 1.25 million immigrants were processed at Ellis Island. Consequently, several hospital buildings, dormitories, contagious disease wards, and kitchens were feverishly constructed between 1900 and 1915.

When the United States entered World War I in 1917 and immigration into the United States decreased, numerous suspected enemy aliens throughout the United States were brought to Ellis Island under custody. At the end of World War I, thousands of suspected alien radicals were interred at Ellis Island. Hun-

dreds were later deported because of their association with organizations advocating revolution against the United States government. However, between 1918 and 1919, detained suspected enemy aliens were transferred from Ellis Island to other locations in order for the United States Navy with the Army Medical Department to take over the island complex for the duration of the war.

During the war, regular inspection of arriving immigrants was conducted on board ship or at the docks, but in 1920, Ellis Island reopened as an immigration receiving station and 225,206 immigrants were processed that year. In the meantime, the immigration restriction legislation that had been passed between 1921 and 1929 during the presidential administrations of Warren Gamaliel Harding and Calvin Coolidge greatly curbed activities at Ellis Island.

After World War I, the United States emerged as a world power. United States

Above: Young boys, the sons of European immigrants, picking slate in a coal breaker in an anthracite mine in Pennsylvania, circa 1913.

Below: This group of immigrants, who arrived at Ellis Island in the 1920s were aided by a YMCA social worker.

Right: Today, Ellis Island appears much as it did to immigrants arriving in the early twentieth century.

embassies were established in countries all over the world, and prospective immigrants now applied for their visas at American consulates in their countries of origin. The necessary paperwork was completed at the consulate and a medical inspection was also conducted there. After 1924, the only people who were detained at Ellis Island were those who had problems with their paperwork, as well as war refugees and displaced persons.

Ellis Island remained open for many years and served a multitude of purposes. For example, during World War II, German and Italian merchant seamen were detained in the Baggage and Dormitory Buildings. The United States Coast Guard also trained about 60,000 servicemen there. In 1954, the last detainee, a Norwegian merchant seaman named Arne Peterssen, was released, and Ellis Island officially closed.

In 1965, President Lyndon Johnson declared Ellis Island part of the Statue of Liberty National Monument, and Ellis Island was opened to the public on a limited basis between

1976 and 1984. Starting in 1984, Ellis Island underwent a major restoration. The Main Building was reopened to the public on September 10, 1990 by the United States Department of the Interior as the Ellis Island Immigration Museum.

The three floors of the Ellis Island Immigration Museum were designed as a self-guided museum. "Island of Hope, Island of Tears," an award winning, 30-minute documentary film is now shown at regularly scheduled times in two theaters. Meanwhile, Living History Programs are offered throughout the spring, summer, and fall. These include a 30-minute play entitled "Ellis Island Stories" that is derived from the oral histories of actual

immigrants that are contained in the museum's oral history collection. Professional actors portray immigrants going through an inspection process at Ellis Island and the experience of immigrating to a strange new place.

The Board of Special Inquiry Program is a living history program which presents the accounts of actual immigrant hearings conducted during the time of peak immigration at Ellis Island. This program is conducted in the "Hearing Room" which has been carefully restored to simulate its appearance in the 1908-1911 period. Audience participation decides the fate of the immigrant standing before an immigration panel, and visitors are shown the importance of immigration policy at the turn of the century and current-day immigration law.

The United States Department of the Interior and the National Park Service — with the collaboration of The National Archives — presents a Genealogy Workshop at Ellis Island for visitors who wish to research their family immigration history. This workshop is offered on a monthly basis and provides instruction about how to gather, interpret, and use historical data to trace family histories.

One of the most popular exhibits at the Ellis Island Immigration Museum is the American Immigrant Wall of Honor. The Wall of Honor is located outdoors, just outside the "Peopling of America" exhibit. The Wall honors America's immigrants regardless of when they immigrated or through which port they entered. The Wall is currently inscribed with over 500,000 names.

The various sections of the Ellis Island complex have been restored to simulate their appearance at various points in the history of the facility as a means of telling the story of Ellis Island. The Baggage Room, restored to simulate the 1918-1924 period, is where thousands of immigrants crowded on a daily basis to check their baggage before climbing the steps to the Registry Room. The Registry Room, restored to simulate the 1918-1924 period, is in the historic Great Hall, which was once filled with new arrivals wait-

ing to be inspected and registered by immigration officers. It now contains historic benches and reproduction inspector desks. The Peopling of America exhibit was originally the Railroad Ticket Office, where immigrants could make travel arrangements to their final destinations in the United States, and it has been restored to simulate the 1918-1924 period. The Dormitory Room on the third floor has been restored and refurbished to replicate the 1908 period.

The Ellis Island Oral History Project, based at the Ellis Island Immigration Museum, is the oldest and largest oral history project dedicated to preserving the first-hand recollections of immigrants coming to America during the years Ellis Island was in operation (1892-1954). Begun in 1973 by National Park Service employee Margo Nash, the Project has grown over the years to include over 1500 interviews. Each interview includes an extensive examination of everyday life in the country of origin, family history, reasons for coming to America, the journey to the port, experiences on the ship, arrival and processing at the Ellis Island facility, and an in-depth look at the adjustment to living in the United States. The present full-time and volunteer staff adds over 100 interviews per year to the collection. All interviews are available as tapes and transcripts to researchers and interested members of the public. The exhibits in the museum rely heavily on quoted oral history material, as does the museum's film created by Charles Guggenheim. Interviews from the Oral History Project have been used extensively in the United States and Europe for television and film documentaries, radio broadcasts, books, creative artwork, and theatrical presentations.

The Ellis Island Oral History Project interviewees are chosen by the Project staff in a number of ways. The most common and useful method is called the "Oral History Form," a simple two-page questionnaire distributed at the museum and through the mail to interested parties. This form asks for an abbreviated immigration history of the potential interviewee with a space to include any other interesting stories or anecdotes. The Project

staff, upon receiving the completed form in the mail, decides if the person would be a good interviewee. Other methods of locating interviewees include the cooperation of ethnic societies and community organizations, newspaper and magazine coverage of the Project, public appearances by the staff, and word of mouth. Once chosen, the interviewee is given the option of coming to the Ellis Island Immigration Museum to be interviewed at the recording studio established by the Hearst Foundation, or having a member of the Project

Above: Unique among the YMCA social workers who aided immigrants at Ellis Island in the 1920s, Ludmilla K. Foxlee liked to dress in central European peasant costume.

staff visit his or her home using portable recording equipment. The running time of most interviews is approximately one hour. Each interviewee is given his or her own copy of the interview on a standard audio cassette as a way of showing appreciation for their time and effort. The interviews are eventually transcribed. Interviews are added to a computer database that can be accessed in the library at the Ellis Island Immigration Museum.

The interviewees include people from dozens of countries, as well as former Ellis Island and Statue of Liberty employees, people stationed in the military on both islands, and former island residents whose family members were employees while they themselves were children. Interviewees presently live in most states in the continental United States, as well as several foreign countries. Most interviewees are in their late 80s, with the oldest being 106 and the youngest, 46.

The library at the Statue of Liberty National Monument and Ellis Island is located on the third floor of the west wing of the Ellis Island Immigration Museum. It is a research library with subject emphasis on the Statue of Liberty, Ellis Island, immigration, and ethnic groups.

The Other Island

While the most important United States immigration station in the early twentieth century was at Ellis Island in the harbor of America's most important city, there were other important stations located on other important islands. The most notable of these was Angel Island in San Francisco Bay, which was the arrival point for over 175,000 people who entered the United States' West Coast between 1910 and 1940. The primary port of entry for Chinese immigrants, Angel Island was virtually identical to Ellis Island, albeit on a smaller scale. The average stay was two weeks, although some Chinese immigrants were held for as long as two years.

The Angel Island Immigration Station stood abandoned from 1940 until 1970, when, as the barracks were about to be torn down, a California State Park ranger discovered Chinese writing on the walls. When the words were translated into English, it was discovered that the writings were poems the immigrants had written to express their fear, anger, and loneliness as they waited there to be

Above: Sampling grapes from push carts in New York City's Little Italy in the early 1930s.

questioned. With the historic importance of the site thus revealed, the state of California made Angel Island into a state park and preserved the buildings.

The Border Patrol

An unintended result of the quota system's limits on immigration was a great rise in illegal immigration by the 1920s. European refugees often migrated first to Canada or Mexico, countries not subject to quotas, and then entered the United States. A whole industry grew up around smuggling illegal aliens. After 1917, a higher head tax and literacy requirement caused more people to try illegal entry. Quota laws of the early 1920s magnified this situation. Every year, more Chinese and European emigrants traveled first to Canada or Mexico, and then illegally crossed the border by land. Many others went first to Cuba, and smugglers brought them from there into the United States by water.

Illegal crossing of the United States' land borders had been a national problem as early as the 1890s. Since then, officers inspected individuals at border crossing stations at specified ports of entry to see that they could legally enter the country. It was illegal to cross the border anywhere other than a port of entry, but people wanting to avoid the exclusions of contract labor laws or the 1891 act often did so.

Efforts to stop smuggling and illegal entries along the southern border date back to 1904. In that year the Commissioner General of Immigration first sent a small group of inspectors to patrol the area on horseback. Ten years later a larger mounted patrol also used automobiles to monitor the boundary. Yet these patrolmen were still Immigrant Inspectors who could not watch the border at all times. Only a permanent force, it seemed, could prevent illegal entries or find and deport illegal aliens. Thus the Department of Labor Appropriation Act passed by the United States Congress, and signed into law by President Calvin Coolidge on May 28, 1924, provided for the establishment of the United States Border Patrol, a law enforcement agency which would be responsible for maintaining control of United States borders by preventing illegal crossings by aliens between the ports of entry.

Below: Cars head south
through the San Ysidro port of
entry between Tijuana,
Mexico and San Diego,
California, sometime during
the 1920s.

Under the jurisdiction of the Bureau of Immigration, the 450 Border Patrol officers evolved from a small cadre of mounted inspectors authorized in 1904 by the Commissioner General of Immigration to patrol the United States-Mexico border. This force of a mere 75 officers was overwhelmed by the number of illegal crossings — especially by smugglers — so the Coolidge Administration acted with characteristic decisiveness.

The early Border Patrol officers, hastily trained and lightly equipped, were given jurisdiction over the 1,945 miles of the Mexican border and 3,987 miles of the Canadian border. In 1925 this area of responsibility was extended to include 2,057 miles of Florida shoreline and the Gulf Coast. In 1930 the United States Border Patrol apprehended 20,915 smuggled aliens and 1,427 assorted criminals on charges ranging from dope smuggling to gun-running, and enforced the notorious Volstead Act which, for more than a decade, inflicted prohibition of alcoholic beverages on the American people.

By the 1930s, along with saddle horses and cars, Border Patrol agents were using trucks, motorboats, and radios in their work. In the 1940s they would add autogiros, airplanes, and eventually helicopters.

The Great Depression

In the late 1920s, as the United States enjoyed unprecedented prosperity and ignored ominous signs of the impending economic collapse that would take place in October 1929, immigration legislation — such as the Registry Act of March 2, 1929 — continued in a restrictive vein by defining classes of acceptability.

On October 29, 1929 — known forever as Black Tuesday — the New York Stock Market collapsed. Panic caused the losses to continue in the following days and weeks, and soon the rest of the United States economy and world markets were pulled down as well. It was an economic disaster of unprecedented magnitude. The collapse continued for three years and took a decade to reverse. One American worker in every four — many of them recent immigrants or sons of immigrants — was out of a job. In other countries, especially those from which the immigrants had come, unemployment remained as high or higher for years. Most European countries were hit hard because they had not yet fully recovered from World War I.

The Great Depression produced millions of unemployed. In the presence of the bread lines, with the terrible burden on private

Above: Immigrant owned pushcarts line the streets in Lower Manhattan, New York City, in the early 1930s.

and public charity, even the legal quotas of immigrants had to be cut off. In 1934, the United States received a total of only 21,000 immigrants, and 80,000 more left United States shores than arrived here.

The earliest immigration legislation that occurred against the backdrop of the Great Depression was an official act passed by the United States Congress, and signed into law by President Herbert Hoover on February 18, 1931. This law, essentially an anti-drug law in the mold of the later twentieth century, provided for the deportation of any alien convicted of violation of United States laws concerning the importation, exportation, manufacture, or sale of heroin, opium, or coca leaves.

The next Depression-era law governing immigration dealt with — as might have been expected — the Contract Labor Laws. Since 1886, performing artists such as actors and singers had been specifically exempted. However, the official act passed by the United States Congress, and signed into law by President Herbert Hoover on March 17, 1932 (on St. Patrick's Day) provided that the Contract Labor Laws were applicable to alien instrumental musicians whether they were entering the United States temporarily or coming for permanent residence.

Under the Act of 1932, such people would not be considered "artists or professional actors" as they had been under the terms of the Immigration Act of 1917. They would specifically not be exempt from the Contract Labor Laws, unless they happened to be "recognized to be of distinguished ability and coming to fulfill professional engagements corresponding to such ability." This left a great deal of leeway in terms of interpretation, but it also had a chilling effect on many individuals. It was hard for many musicians to accept the qualifications of a Bureau of Immigration official to determine whether he or she was of "distinguished ability."

The Act of March 17, 1932 went on to state that if the alien did qualify for exemption under the "distinguished ability" proviso, the Secretary of Labor — or his Bureau of Immigration designees — would have the authority to require such conditions as bonding to insure that the alien musician would actually *leave* the United States after his or her engagement was concluded.

The Contract Labor Laws continued to be on the minds of Congress and the Hoover Administration through 1932. It was an election year occurring against the backdrop of the worst unemployment in modern history, and there was a groundswell of sentiment that opposed continued immigration of foreign contract laborers when millions of Americans — many of them foreign-born naturalized Americans — were out of work.

The second act of 1932 that amended Contract Labor Law was passed by the United States Congress and signed into law by President Hoover on May 2. It specifically amended the Immigration Act of 1917 through doubling the allocation for enforcement of the Contract Labor Laws. Close on its heels was the act passed by Congress and signed into law by the President on July 1. This act amended the Immigration Act of 1924, providing that the specified classes of nonimmigrant aliens could be admitted for a prescribed period of time, *but* under such conditions (including bonding where deemed necessary) that would ensure their departure at the expiration of their "prescribed time" or if they failed to maintain the status under which admitted. In other words, the July 1 law did to many classes of aliens what

the "St. Patrick's Day law" had done to musicians.

The official act passed by the United States Congress and signed into law by President Hoover on July 11, 1932 actually provided exemption from quota limits to certain people. Specifically, the new law accorded "nonquota status" to the husbands of American citizens, provided that the marriage had occurred "prior to issuance of the visa and prior to July 1, 1932." Meanwhile, wives of citizens were accorded nonquota status regardless of the time of marriage.

During the Great Depression, immigration laws provided for the deportation of "public charges" and vagrants under certain conditions. America was no longer "the land of promise." William Nuckles Doak — a former official of the Brotherhood of Railroad Trainmen — who served as the United States Secretary of Labor at the end of the Herbert Hoover presidential administration, had a clearly defined policy of deportation. First, Doak had publicly announced that he intended to rid the country of undesirable foreigners. In some instances, he employed the "anarchist," or radical, clause of the immigration law, but he also made a drive against vagrants and the unemployed, as well as those present in the United States illegally.

In his memoirs, Edward Corsi, the former United States Commissioner for Immigration and Naturalization for the New York District, tells of a particularly illustrative incident. At one point in 1930, the New York Police Department Alien Squadron, accompanied by federal immigration inspectors detailed by Secretary Doak to Ellis Island, entered a Finnish dance hall in Harlem. They locked the doors behind them and lined the people against the walls and searched them. Those who could not convince the officers that they were in the country legally were arrested. A repetition of this event occurred at the Seamen's Home on South Street. Seamen, many of whom claimed to be American citizens and some of whom were later released, were roused from their beds and taken to Ellis Island.

The changing tide of immigration brought about by the Great Depression is illustrated by the fact that in 1928, there were 307,355 immigrants versus 77,457 emigrants, and in 1931, there were 97,139 immigrants versus 61,882 emigrants, while in 1933, there were only 23,068 immigrants and 127,660 emigrants.

The year 1932 was the actual changing of the tide. It was the first year in more than a century that more people (103,295) left United States shores than were arriving (35,576).

Immigration policy was not a key issue, however, in the election of 1932. The key issue was that the United States was still in the depths of the Great Depression, and it seemed to voters that the Hoover Administration was utterly powerless to do anything to improve the economy or the plight of the American people. Millions had lost their jobs, savings, and homes. During the time that Hoover was in office, the shares of industrial companies had lost 80 percent of their pre-1929 value and roughly 11,000 banks had failed, taking with them $2 billion in deposits. Whereas President Hoover opposed government intervention in the economy, his challenger in the 1932 election promised just the opposite.

Early Roosevelt Era Immigration Policy

Former New York Governor Franklin Delano Roosevelt was elected President by a wide margin to ease the mounting economic distress through his activist New Deal economic plan. The New Deal was an umbrella for many programs and an extensive list of new agencies. Roosevelt's National Recovery Administration was based on the notion of wage and price stabilization, but it was abandoned after the Supreme Court declared it to be unconstitutional in 1935. However, the New Deal did expand United States federal government relief efforts and job-creating projects, such as the Public Works Administration and the Civilian Conservation Corps.

In terms of immigration policy, the Democratic Roosevelt Administration did not, as some might have predicted, take a much different approach than had the Republican Coolidge and Hoover Administrations. The first immigration law of the Roosevelt Administration was not actually passed until the third year of his first term. This official act passed by the United States Congress, and signed into law by President Roosevelt on June 15, 1935, was considered a protective measure for American seamen. It repealed the laws giving privi-

leges of citizenship regarding service on and protection by American vessels to aliens who had made declaration of intent to become American citizens, who were, in the vernacular of the times, said to have received their "first papers."

Early in President Roosevelt's second term, steps were taken to further tighten immigration by further expanding the classes of deportable aliens. The official act passed by the United States Congress, and signed into law by President Roosevelt on May 14, 1937, was addressed at "marriages of convenience," and made deportable any alien who was, after entering the United States, found to have secured a visa through fraud by contracting a marriage which after his or her entry into the United States had been "judicially annulled retroactively to the date of the marriage," or if an alien had failed or refused to fulfill his or her "promises for a marital agreement" made to gain entry as an immigrant.

The Depression decade of 1931-1940 saw just 528,431 immigrants, the lowest num-

Above: Elected President in 1932, Franklin Delano Roosevelt favored active government involvement in the economy, and — during his first term — restrictive immigration policies.

ber of any decade since the 1820s and just six percent of the immigration experienced in the first decade of the twentieth century. Of this total, the largest number — 114,058 — came from Germany, which was embracing Nazism. Canadians were next, with 108,527, followed by 68,028 Italians.

Meanwhile, the Immigration Bureau underwent reorganization, reform, and rapid change during the first decade of the Roosevelt Administration. Executive Order 6166 of June 10, 1933 again combined the Immigration Bureau and the Naturalization Bureau and placed both functions within the Department of Labor. It has since been known as the Immigration and Naturalization Service (INS). The purpose of this reorganization was to bring naturalization under more centralized control. The Immigration and Naturalization Service Central Office set standard naturalization procedures, and in 1934 the Secretary of Labor selected an Ellis Island Committee to study naturalization and immigration problems and to suggest reforms.

There were fewer entries and a smaller alien population than in earlier years. In fact, during the early 1930s immigration fell to a record low and emigration climbed to a record high. Yet many Americans in the 1930s clung to the idea that the nation was drowning in a flood of immigrants. The committee's report led to various laws regarding, among other things, naturalization and nationality, deportation, and suspension of deportation.

Though the United States had asserted its right to deport aliens since 1798, deportation was rare through most of the nineteenth century. Only when federal immigration law created exclusions during the late nineteenth century, and increased the number of grounds for exclusion, did deportation come into use as a way to enforce immigration laws. Steamship and railroad companies began to inspect passengers because United States law required them to provide return passage for any excludable aliens. The immigration law of 1891 specified that deportation could occur only within one year after entry, but this limit grew over time. By 1924 the limit on deportability became five years for most violations, while for others there was no time after which deportation was impossible.

The lower tide of immigration would soon change. Increasing numbers of refugees applied for admission to the United States as Europe experienced economic depression and the rise of fascism in the 1930s. In 1938, Adolf Hitler invaded Austria and sparked further movement of refugees and displaced persons that would continue to grow in the postwar period. Yet the Quota Act allowed only a few of these people to immigrate to the United States in the 1930s, far fewer than the number that applied.

Naturalizations increased during the Great Depression. Immigrants mainly had economic reason to naturalize in these years, as citizens were hired first in a country where jobs were scarce. Also, benefits from many social programs created by the New Deal went only to citizens. Naturalization work expanded, so the Immigration and Naturalization Service built a special unit to investigate naturalization fraud. Though able to eliminate most fraud and corruption, the unit found few uniform naturalization practices across the country.

Rapid changes in transportation challenged immigration inspection work in the 1930s. Historically, the vast majority of people entered the country at seaports, where ships landed daily during regular business hours. With the growing use of cars on new highways, there were now more land ports than seaports. Furthermore, land ports were open 24 hours a day and created a need for more Inspectors and Border Patrol Agents. By the end of the decade, the INS began preparing for changes in international air travel as well.

World War II Emergency Immigration Policy

Whereas most previous legislation had dealt with immigration as an internal economic or political issue, the beginning of World War II saw the United States Congress and President Roosevelt turning their attention to immigration laws and restrictions as a means of protecting the United States from subversive elements. The United States would not actually become a combatant in World War II for over two years, but it was clear to most people where the threat lay, and that was with the Axis powers, particularly Nazi Germany.

The election year of 1940 saw the biggest surge of immigration legislation in history, rivaling even the election year of 1924, when Calvin Coolidge was up for reelection. The election year of 1940 also took place against the backdrop of World War II, which had been raging in Europe since September 1939. In the space of a few months in the spring of 1940, the German armies had conquered Norway, Denmark, Belgium, the Netherlands, and France. The Battle of Britain had begun with massive air attacks, and many people predicted the demise of that nation by the end of the year.

It had also been revealed that in the defeat of many of the occupied European nations, the Germans had used subversive agents disguised as immigrants or aliens. With the shadow of Nazi tyranny looming toward the Western Hemisphere, it did not take a stretch of the imagination to see that immigration policy would play an important role in keeping the United States safe from Nazi subversion. Many of the immigration laws enacted during 1940 dealt with this problem. The first, passed by the United States Congress and signed into law by President Roosevelt on June 14, 1940, was known as Presidential Reorganization Plan Number V. Under this plan, the Immigration and Naturalization Service was transferred from the Department of Labor to the Department of

Justice as a national security measure. Transfer to an enforcement agency was a logical step. Before and during the war the Immigration and Naturalization Service cooperated with other agencies, such as the Federal Bureau of Investigation, when dealing with alien enemies or subversives. Once at war, Congress passed a series of acts intended to provide more control of aliens in the United States.

Two weeks later, as France fell to the German armies, Congress passed the Alien Registration Act of 1940, which was signed by the President on June 28. Since 1845 there had been attempts in the United States to create or require a record of aliens within the country. A 1906 law even mandated beginning such a registry, but not until the Alien Registration Act of 1940, passed as a war measure, did a registry come into existence. It required registration of all aliens and fingerprinting of those over 14 years of age, and established additional deportable classes, including aliens convicted of smuggling, or assisting in the illegal entry of, other aliens. Dealing boldly and directly with the possibility of internal subver-

Above: President Roosevelt signing the Declaration of War in December 1941. Among the emergency measures that were already in effect was the Public Safety Act of 1941, which officially directed consular officers to refuse visas to any aliens seeking to enter the United States for the purpose of engaging in activities which would endanger the safety of the United States.

sion, the Alien Registration Act amended the October 16, 1919 law that had made *present* membership in subversive organizations grounds for exclusion and deportation by now also making *past* membership in such groups grounds for exclusion and deportation. High on the list of such groups was, of course, the Nazi Party.

Another important wartime immigration measure that was passed that week and signed into law by President Roosevelt on July 1, 1940, amended the Immigration Act of 1924 by requiring aliens admitted as officials of foreign governments to maintain their status or depart.

The Nationality Act of 1940, which was passed by Congress and signed into law by President Roosevelt on October 14, codified and revised the naturalization, citizenship, and expatriation laws to strengthen the national defense. Becoming effective on January 13, 1941, it provided for the rewriting of naturalization and nationality regulations, as well as revising the forms used in naturalization proceedings.

America's involvement in World War II heightened national security concerns in all branches of government. The Immigration and Naturalization Service detained and interned enemy aliens throughout the war, and efforts to identify and monitor the United States' alien population began in these years. Following the war's end, Cold War concerns influenced the admission of refugees, as well as revision of the law into the Immigration and Nationality Act of 1952.

The Alien Registration Act of 1940 worked to deport more subversives, and made failure to register under the act a new ground for deportation. This law codified voluntary departure, a practice that would come into greater use in the 1940s and after when the number of illegal entries began to grow. By the late 1940s deportation procedures became more costly and time consuming. Under voluntary departure aliens agreed to return to their home countries at their own expense, thus avoiding a record of deportation. Many chose this option because deportation would exclude them from future legal admission to the United States for five years, while voluntary departure had no such ban.

Aliens who did not admit being excludable, and therefore deportable, could now appeal an exclusion or deportation order. Only after a fair hearing before a special inquiry officer, called an "Immigration Judge," could an alien now be deported. At deportation hearings aliens were now entitled to such considerations as notification of charges against them, legal representation, a chance to confront evidence against them, and the opportunity to present witnesses or evidence on their behalf.

If, after the hearing, the order of deportation remained, the alien was now permitted to appeal the decision to the newly created Board of Immigration Appeals. Earlier in the century, in the 1920s, there had been so many appeals to the Secretary of Labor that he had established a Board of Review to help him decide all the cases. When the Service transferred to the Department of Justice in 1940, the Board of Review became the Board of Immigration Appeals, which became separate from the Immigration and Naturalization Service within the Justice Department.

Passed by Congress and signed into law on June 20, 1941, the landmark Public Safety Act of 1941 officially directed consular officers to refuse visas to any aliens seeking to enter the United States for the purpose of engaging in activities which would endanger the safety of the United States. The following day, President Roosevelt signed a law which officially extended the World War I emergency Act of May 22, 1918, which gave a president the power — during a time of national emergency or war — to prevent an alien from entering or leaving the United States if such a transit was deemed contrary to public safety.

While Nazi agents were indeed quite active in the United States, the catalyst that brought the United States into World War II was not subversion from Nazi Germany, but

rather an overt military act of war on the part of one of Nazi Germany's close allies. The December 7, 1941 attack by the Japanese Imperial Navy on the American naval base at Pearl Harbor in Hawaii cost the lives of 2,400 Americans, many of them civilians, but it also mobilized United States public opinion against the Japanese and resulted in a declaration of war the following day. In asking Congress for the declaration, President Roosevelt said "December 7, 1941 is a date which will live in infamy."

No specific United States federal immigration legislation was passed as a result of Pearl Harbor, but emergency measures were taken to round up Japanese agents in the western states. However, these measures were undertaken much too zealously, and American citizens of Japanese ancestry were interned for the duration of the war under the mistaken belief that they bore a stronger allegiance to Japan than to the United States.

The Immigration and Naturalization Service operated several detention centers and internment camps for enemy aliens throughout the war as part of its duty to monitor aliens resident in the United States. The Service deported some enemy aliens, paroled some, and detained or interned others for the duration of the war. The Immigration and Naturalization Service detained Germans and Italians at the camps, but the overwhelming majority of internees were Japanese, or of Japanese descent. When internment camps opened during World War II, Americans feared a West Coast invasion by Japan. It was not until 40 years later that the United States government finally investigated whether internment had been justified.

The first United States immigration legislation passed after the United States entry into World War II was signed into law by President Roosevelt on December 8, 1942, the first anniversary of the official start of the war. It amended the Immigration Act of 1917, altering the reporting procedure in suspension of deportation cases to require the Attorney General to report such suspensions to Congress on the first and fifteenth of each month that Congress is in session.

While the clearly reprehensible internment of Japanese-Americans is often viewed through hindsight as a racist act, it was more an overreaction to the Japanese attack on United States territory. This is evidenced by the simultaneous embrace of the cause of China — which itself had been the victim of a brutal

invasion by the Japanese Imperial Army. Not only did the United States government actively support the Chinese war effort with supplies and United States troops, there were many successful campaigns to raise money to supply food and humanitarian aid to the Chinese people.

In terms of immigration policy, it is significant that on December 17, 1943 President Roosevelt signed an amendment to the Alien Registration Act of 1940 which added Chinese persons and persons of Chinese descent to the classes eligible for naturalization. This amendment officially repealed the Chinese Exclusion laws, which dated back to, and even before the Act of May 6, 1882.

The repeal in 1943 of the controversial Chinese Exclusion Acts made Chinese immigrants eligible for naturalization, although potential immigrants had to be eligible for United States citizenship to get visas. In 1946, Congress extended eligibility for citizenship to natives of India and the Philippines. Before, only Filipinos who served in the United States military could gain citizenship. Naturalizations increased during the war, due in part to the number of aliens who earned citizenship by serving in the United States armed

Above: A Japanese-American child awaiting transportation to an internment camp in early 1942. The internment of Japanese-American citizens as national security risks is one of the darkest moments in the history of United States policy toward immigrants and their American-born descendants.

forces. New naturalized citizens came from Europe, Africa, the South Pacific, and elsewhere.

The Bracero Program

There is perhaps no more striking illustration of how far the United States economy improved between 1933 and 1943 than the Bracero Program. In 1933, the United States economy had collapsed upon itself. Unemployment had soared to frightening levels and deflation had decimated the wages of those Americans who still clung to their jobs. By 1943, thanks in no small part to World War II, the economy was booming and unemployment had vanished. Unemployment had evaporated to the point where women not only had the opportunity for high-paid industrial jobs, they were very much in demand. In the agricultural sector there were so few workers for the massive number of available jobs that the United States had to import workers.

It is an interesting irony that, while immigration laws had been designed for generations to *restrict* immigration and contract labor, by 1943, laws had to be written to *encourage* immigration and contract labor. Such was the Bracero Program.

The Bracero Program was established by the United States Congress and signed into being by President Roosevelt on April 29, 1943. The program provided for the importation of temporary agricultural laborers

into the United States from North, South, and Central America to aid agriculture during World War II.

Meanwhile, the official act passed by the United States Congress, and signed into law by President Roosevelt on February 14, 1944, provided for the importation of temporary workers from countries in the Western Hemisphere pursuant to agreements with such countries for employment in industries and services essential to the war efforts. Agreements were subsequently made with British Honduras (now Belize), Jamaica, Barbados, and the British West Indies.

Though it has occasionally been criticized in hindsight, the Bracero Program was a classic win-win situation. It provided agricultural workers at reasonable cost during a critical labor shortage, and it also provided jobs to Latin Americans at a much higher pay scale than was available at the time in Latin America. An estimated half million Latin American farm laborers came north annually to work in the rich agricultural land of the United States, primarily in the harvesting of vegetables and the picking of cotton. The Bracero Program was later extended through 1947, and the Agricultural Act of October 31, 1949 would extend it for more than a decade.

Further immigration legislation involving farm workers included the official act passed by the United States Congress, and signed into law by President Truman on June 30, 1950, which provided relief to the sheepherding industry by authorizing that, during a one-year period, 250 special quota immigration visas could be issued to skilled sheepherders, with these visas being chargeable to oversubscribed quotas. The official act passed by the United States Congress and signed into law by President Harry S. Truman on April 9, 1952, provided that an additional 500 immigration visas could be issued to sheepherders. On September 3, 1954, President Dwight Eisenhower signed a law that made special nonquota immigrant visas available to certain skilled sheepherders for a period of up to one year. Because petty violations of local laws were occasionally used as grounds to deport foreign agricultural workers, the 1954 law also exempted from inadmissibility to the United States aliens who had committed no more than one such petty offense.

Meanwhile, the Agricultural Act of 1949 was amended in 1951 by the official act passed by the United States Congress, and signed into law by President Truman on July 12 of that year. This law not only amended the Agricultural Act of 1949, it served as the basic framework under which the Mexican Bracero Program operated until 1962. The 1951 law provided that the United States government would establish and operate reception centers at or near the Mexican border. The United States government would also provide transportation, subsistence, and medical care from the Mexican recruiting centers to the United States reception centers and guarantee performance by employers in matters relating to transportation and wages, including all forms of remuneration.

The 1951 law also required United States employers to pay the prevailing wages in the area, to guarantee the workers employment for three-fourths of the contract period, and to provide workers with free housing and adequate meals at a reasonable cost.

The final official act regarding the Bracero Program was passed by the United States Congress and signed into law by President Lyndon Johnson on December 13, 1963. Under this law, the Mexican Bracero Program was extended one additional year to December 31, 1964, when it officially ended after 21 years.

Postwar Immigration Policy

World War II ended in 1945 with the May 7 surrender of Nazi Germany and the September 3 surrender of the Japanese Empire. World War II brought global population shifts and change to the United States and many other countries throughout the world. The United States government grew in size during the war years, and the Immigration and Naturalization Service shared in that expansion.

Not only were new units created within the Service, but the number of employees more than doubled, jumping from about 1,000 to 8,500 in just two years.

The United States discovered new obligations and problems as it emerged as a superpower in 1945. As the nation converted back to peacetime after World War II, many of the old immigration laws were clearly inadequate or obsolete. During 1946, admissions reached 108,721 persons, more than had arrived in 16 years. Meanwhile, illegal entries were higher than ever before in history. The American public soon became concerned, even fearful, about the large number of refugees and displaced persons seeking to move from Europe to the United States.

There is a long tradition in America of welcoming people who flee or have fled persecution, war, or natural disaster. Through colonial times and most of the nineteenth century there were no restrictive immigration laws. Therefore there was no need for refugee policy or laws of asylum. By the 1940s, United States laws limiting immigration lacked a mechanism to deal with the numbers of refugees fleeing Europe.

President Harry Truman began to face the issue of European refugees in December of 1945. A Presidential Directive of December 22, 1945 allowed the admission of 40,000 refugees outside the immigration laws.

The wartime fears and urgencies also gave way to new issues. In terms of immigration policy, this would involve dealing with new classes of immigrants. Because many United States service personnel stationed overseas — primarily in Great Britain — during World War II had married foreign nationals and wanted to bring them to live in the United States, it was necessary to create a means to nationalize these persons.

The result was the War Brides Act of 1945, signed into law by President Harry Truman on December 28 of that year. The War Brides Act — so named because the vast majority of the foreign nationals *were* brides — waived visa requirements and provisions of immigration law excluding physical and mental defectives in the case of persons who had married members of the American armed forces during World War II. The War Brides Act of 1945 was further expanded though the GI Fiancees Act of 1946, which was signed into law by President Harry Truman on June 29, and which facilitated the admission into the United States of fiancees of members of the American armed forces.

The United States Congress continued in this vein with the passage of a series of similar laws over the coming months. On August 9, 1946, President Truman signed the law which gave nonquota status to Chinese wives of American citizens. This was followed by the law signed on June 28, 1947 which extended by six months the Attorney General's authority to admit alien fiancees of

Above: A Mexican man at work in Robson, Texas under the Bracero Program.

Below: Gustav Worke immigrated to the United States in 1912 and was an American citizen through two world wars which pitted his nation of origin against his adopted land. He was photographed on his farm near Southington, Connecticut in 1942 by Fenno Jacobs.

veterans as temporary visitors pending marriage. In 1950, an official act passed by the United States Congress, and signed into law by President Truman on August 19 of that year would make spouses and minor children of members of the American armed forces — regardless of the alien's race — eligible for immigration and nonquota status, providing that the the marriage had occurred before March 19, 1952.

Immigration policy history was made on December 17, 1943, when President Roosevelt signed the amendment to the Alien Registration Act of 1940, which effectively repealed the Chinese Exclusion laws which dated back to and before the Act of May 6, 1882. This momentum continued in the postwar years when Congress amended the Immigration Act of 1917 to expand immigration from India and the Philippines. This act was, in turn, signed into law by President Truman on July 2, 1946.

As noted above, a major international issue coming out of World War II was that of war refugees, or in the vernacular of the times, "displaced persons." To provide further relief to emigres fleeing war-ravaged areas, Congress in 1948 passed the Displaced Persons Act. This law operated outside the immigration selection system of the Immigration and Nationality Act. Extended until 1952 and executed by the Displaced Persons Commission, the Displaced Persons Act ultimately allowed the admission of over 390,000 people to the United States. To protect the national origins system of the United States' immigration police, the Displaced Persons Act allowed these entries by mortgaging country quotas into the future.

The Displaced Persons Act signed into law by President Truman on June 25, 1948 was the first expression of United States policy for admitting persons fleeing persecution. It permitted the admission of up to 205,000 displaced persons during the two-year period beginning July 1, 1948, chargeable against a future year's quotas. The Displaced Persons Act of 1948 was aimed at reducing the problem created by the presence in Germany, Austria, and Italy of more than a million people who had been uprooted from their native lands by World War II and the subsequent brutal occupation of eastern Europe by the forces of the Soviet Red Army.

The Displaced Persons Act of 1948 was amended by Congress in 1950. In a law signed by President Truman on June 16, 1950, the amendments to the Displaced Persons Act extended the act to June 30, 1951 and extended its application to war orphans, "expellees" from the Soviet occupied eastern part of Germany, and refugees to July 1, 1952. The 1950 law increased the total number of persons who could be admitted under the Displaced Persons Act of 1948 from 205,000 to 415,744.

During the second world war — because of national security issues — immigration into the United States was at its lowest level since the 1820s, and was lower even than during the Great Depression. After the war, immigration began to rise steadily, although the annual totals would not reach pre-Depression levels until the 1980s. During the 1940s, a total of 1,035,039 immigrants entered the United States. The largest nationality group was the 226,578 immigrants who arrived from Germany after World War II, followed by 171,718 who arrived from Canada and 139,306 who immigrated from the United Kingdom.

Cold War Immigration Policy

Soviet aggressiveness and implied threat of military attack on western Europe, as manifested by such actions as the 1948-1949 Berlin Blockade, were the beginnings of four decades of international tension that would be known as the Cold War. The Soviet military build-up was accompanied by covert and overt subversive operations in western Europe and other parts of the world. This was clearly reminiscent of the events leading up to Nazi aggression prior to and during World War II.

After a brief moment of postwar euphoria, the United States was compelled to face the Soviet threat as it had the Nazi threat — through a defensive military build-up and through immigration legislation aimed at protecting the United States from subversion. The official act passed by the United States Congress, and signed into law by President Truman on May 25, 1948, amended the Act of October 16, 1918 to provide for the expulsion and exclusion of anarchists and similar classes of aliens. The 1948 law gave the Attorney General powers of exclusion that were similar to those the Secretary of State had through the refusal of immigration visas.

A month later, Congress passed and President Truman signed into law (on July 1, 1948) a measure which amended the Immigration Act of 1917 by making it easier for certain aliens to defend themselves against deportation. This new law made possible the suspension of deportation of aliens even though they were ineligible for naturalization by reason of race. The 1948 law also set conditions for suspension of deportation proceedings for any alien who had been of "good moral character for the preceding five years, and that the Attorney General finds that deportation would result in serious economic detriment to a citizen or legal resident and closely related alien, or the alien has resided continuously in the United States for seven years or more."

In 1949, immigration legislation was enacted on behalf of the United States Central Intelligence Agency. In the climate of the Cold War, the United States undertook many activities, both overt and covert, to combat subversive and espionage efforts against the United States by Soviet and other Communist governments. One of these activities was the creation of the Central Intelligence Agency to both gather intelligence and undertake covert operations. In the execution of its duties, the Central Intelligence Agency frequently needed to use foreign operatives, and to protect these persons by allowing them a safe haven in the United States. The Central Intelligence Agency Act of 1949, passed by Congress and signed into law by President Truman on June 20, authorized the admission of a limited number of aliens in the interest of national security.

The Central Intelligence Agency Act of 1949 also provided that whenever the Director of the Central Intelligence Agency, the Attorney General, and the Commissioner of Immigration determined that the entry of a particular alien into the United States for permanent residence was "in the interest of national security or essential to the furtherance of the national intelligence mission, such alien and his immediate family may be given entry into the United States for permanent residence without regard to their admissibility under any laws and regulations or to their failure to comply with such laws and regulations pertaining to admissibility." The number was not to exceed 100 persons per year.

The immigration aspect of the subversion problem within the United States was dealt with by the Internal Security Act of 1950, signed into law by President Truman on September 22 of that year. This law amended various immigration laws with a view toward strengthening security screening in cases of aliens in the United States or applying for entry. The Internal Security Act of 1950 provided that present and former membership in the Communist party — or any other totalitarian party or its affiliates — was specifically a ground for inadmissibility. The act also stated that aliens in the United States who, at the time of their entry or by reason of subsequent actions, would have been inadmissible under the provisions of the Internal Security Act, were made deportable regardless of the length of their residence in the United States.

The Internal Security Act of 1950 noted that any alien deportable as a subversive criminal — or member of what it called "the immoral classes" — who willfully failed to depart from the United States within six months after the issuance of the deportation

Above: President Truman with Soviet leader Josef Stalin (left) at Potsdam, Germany immediately after World War II. Relations between the United States and the Soviet Union deteriorated into the Cold War, which compelled the United States to introduce restrictive immigration policies in the interest of national security.

Below: British Prime Minister Clement Atlee, President Harry Truman and Soviet leader Josef Stalin. Relations between these wartime allies disintegrated in the late 1940s and teetered on the brink of war for more than four decades. In the United States, laws such as the Internal Security Act of 1950 restricted entry into the United States by members of the Communist Party.

order was made liable to criminal prosecution and could be imprisoned for up to 10 years. Every alien residing in the United States who was subject to alien registration was required to notify the Commissioner of Immigration and Naturalization of his or her address within 10 days of each January 1st in which he or she resided in the United States.

Meanwhile, the discretion of the Attorney General in admitting otherwise inadmissible aliens temporarily — and in some instances permanently — was curtailed or eliminated by the Internal Security Act of 1950. However, the Attorney General was given authority to exclude and deport without a hearing an alien whose admission would be prejudicial to the public interest if the Attorney General's finding was based on confidential information, the disclosure of which would have been prejudicial to the public interest of the United States.

Under the Internal Security Act of 1950 the Attorney General was given authority to supervise deportable aliens pending their deportation, and also was given greater latitude in selecting the country of deportation. However, it was prohibited to deport an alien to any country in which the alien would be subject to physical persecution.

While in hindsight the threat of Communism seems somewhat benign, during the 1950s, the United States was operating against the backdrop of the Soviet Union's stated policy of encouraging the overthrow of world governments by violent revolution. Furthermore, the memories of the success of Nazi subversion in Europe in 1940 was still fresh in the memories of policy-makers, especially those who drafted immigration legislation. Thus it was

that legislation was strict in regard to control of Communist activities.

The official act passed by the United States Congress, and signed into law by President Truman on March 28, 1951 gave the Attorney General authority to amend the record of certain aliens who were admitted only temporarily because of affiliations other than Communist. This law also interpreted the act of October 16, 1918 regarding exclusion and expulsion of aliens to include only voluntary membership or affiliation with a Communist organization, and to exclude cases where the person in question was under 16 years of age, or where he or she had joined the Communist Party of a given foreign power simply for the purpose of obtaining employment, food rations, or other necessities.

While the Cold War necessitated immigration law with regard to European aliens, the land borders of the United States continued to be subject to penetration by illegal aliens, and especially by those who profited by clandestinely transporting them into the United States — frequently crammed into inhumane crevices, such as beneath the floorboards of trucks. The official act passed by the United States Congress, and signed into law by President Truman on March 20, 1952 amended the Immigration Act of 1917, making it a felony to bring in or willfully induce an alien unlawfully to enter or reside in the United States. However, under the 1952 law, the usual and normal practices incident to employment were not deemed to constitute harboring. The 1952 law also further defined the powers of the United States Border Patrol, giving officers of the Immigration and Naturalization Service authority to have access to private lands — but not dwellings — within 25 miles of an external boundary for the purpose of patrolling the border to prevent the illegal entry of aliens.

The Immigration and Nationality Act of 1952

For most of the first half of the twentieth century — through two World Wars and the Great Depression — United States immigration policy was largely determined by the sweeping omnibus of the Immigration Act of 1917, along with the National Origins Quota System established by the Immigration Act of 1924 and subsequent modifying or amending legislation.

In the aftermath of World War II and against the backdrop of the Cold War and an

era of dramatically increasing prosperity, Congress undertook to rewrite and redefine United States immigration law as never before. Between 1947 and 1950, the Senate Judiciary Committee investigated the immigration and naturalization system, policy, enforcement, and administration. The committee advised revising and rewriting existing laws regarding immigration. The result was the milestone Immigration and Nationality Act, passed on June 27, 1952. Known familiarly as the INA, the Immigration and Nationality Act of 1952 brought into one comprehensive statute the multiple laws which, before its enactment, governed immigration and naturalization in the United States.

In general, the INA perpetuated the immigration policies from earlier statutes, but there were several significant modifications. Specifically, the INA of 1952 made all races eligible for naturalization, thus eliminating race as a bar to immigration, and it eliminated discrimination between sexes with respect to immigration.

The new law revised the national origins quota system of the Immigration Act of 1924 by changing the national origins quota formula. It set the annual quota for an area at one-sixth of one percent of the number of inhabitants in the continental United States in 1920 whose ancestry or national origin was attributable to that area. All countries were allowed a minimum quota of 100, with a ceiling of 2,000 on most natives of countries in the Asia-Pacific triangle, which broadly encompassed the Asian countries.

At the same time, the law broadened the grounds for exclusion and deportation of aliens, provided procedures for the adjustment of status of nonimmigrant aliens to that of permanent resident aliens, modified and added significantly to the existing classes of non immigrant admission, and afforded greater procedural safeguards to aliens subject to deportation. Repealed by the law was the ban on contract labor contained in the act of March 30, 1868.

The INA of 1952 provided a complete revision of the naturalization and nationality laws. While petitioners for naturalization still had to prove they could read, write, and speak the English language, there were exemptions for elderly people, long-time United States residents, or those with relevant disabilities. A declaration of intention was no longer required for naturalization, though lawfully admitted aliens could make a declaration if they wanted the record for another purpose.

Conditions for gaining and keeping United States citizenship by citizens' children born abroad also changed with the 1952 act. The law set new rules and criteria for United States nationals living abroad regarding dual citizenship and loss of citizenship. Finally, it revised the grounds for canceling citizenship, and added new grounds involving conduct of a subversive nature and adverse to the interests of the United States.

Many Americans opposed the 1952 act because it did not really change the restrictive policy. President Harry Truman vetoed the bill because it, like the old 1924 act, was based on national origins. After Congress overrode his veto on December 24, 1952, President Truman named a special commission to study the weaknesses of the INA law. The commission's 1953 report urged replacement of the national origins system, and suggested instead a system based on reunification of families or upon skills needed by the United States.

The new law revised the preference structure by creating separate categories for skilled workers and for relatives of citizens and

Above: Lines of automobiles waiting to cross the border between San Ysidro, California and Tijuana, Mexico. During the 1950s, illegal crossings of the southern border of the United States began to become a problem that would eventually grow into a serious national immigration policy concern.

87

resident aliens. It expanded security procedures and investigation of immigrants and aliens. It also removed all racial barriers to naturalization, and granted the same preference to husbands as it did to wives of citizens.

The INA of 1952 introduced a system of selected immigration by giving a quota preference to skilled aliens whose services were urgently needed in the United States and to relatives of United States citizens and aliens. The law also placed a limit on the use of the governing country's quota by natives of colonies and dependent areas, and it provided an "escape clause" permitting the immigration of certain former voluntary members of proscribed organizations.

The law introduced the alien address report system, whereby all aliens in the United States (including most temporary visitors) were required to report annually their current address to the Immigration and Naturalization Service. It also established a central index of all aliens in the United States for use by security and enforcement agencies.

Some 1952 changes regarding exclusion were American reactions to the Cold War. Hundreds of thousands of displaced persons and refugees had come to the United States after World War II from Communist countries. This

encouraged American fears of Communism both abroad and at home. Despite new elements to immigration law, the 1952 act — like those of 1917 and 1924 — retained restrictions based on national origin.

The alien registration system begun during World War II became permanent under the 1952 INA. The new law called for registration upon obtaining an immigrant visa. Between 1952 and 1981, aliens present in the United States were also required to file annual address reports.

The Eisenhower Years

Sworn in as the 34th United States president on January 20, 1953, Dwight Eisenhower came to the office after a distinguished military career, during which time he was promoted to five-star rank to serve as Supreme Commander of Allied Forces in Europe during World War II, and later as military commander of all North Atlantic Treaty Organization (NATO) forces and as Chief of Staff of the United States Army.

Upon taking office in 1953, President Eisenhower called for Congress to review the immigration and nationality law to eliminate its injustices. He reiterated this recommendation throughout his two terms. Limited reform came during a decade of specific legislation designed to remedy defects in the INA of 1952. It would not be until 1965 that major amendments to the act abandoned the old national origins system. During Eisenhower's eight-year tenure as President, immigration legislation continued to follow in the national security theme of the earlier Cold War years, with some general legislation to amend and expand the provisions codified in the INA of 1952.

As an example of the former type of law, the official act passed by the United States Congress, and signed into law by President Eisenhower on September 3, 1954, provided for the expatriation of persons convicted of engaging in a conspiracy to overthrow or levy war against the United States government. However, the act passed by Congress, and signed by President Eisenhower on July 24, 1957, permitted enlistment of aliens into the regular United States Army. This situation was modified by the official act passed by the United States Congress, and signed into law by President John F. Kennedy on August 17, 1961, which provided that, in peacetime, no volunteer is to be accepted into the United

States Army or United States Air Force unless the person is a citizen or an alien admitted for permanent residence.

An example of more general Eisenhower-era immigration legislation was the act passed by Congress and signed into law by President Eisenhower on August 30, 1957, which exempted aliens who were survivors of certain deceased members of the United States armed forces from provisions of the Social Security Act which prohibited the payment of benefits to aliens outside the United States.

Possibly the most important immigration law enacted during the Eisenhower Administration was the Refugee-Escapee Act of 1957 that was signed by President Eisenhower on September 11 of that year. This law addressed the problem of quota oversubscription by removing the "mortgaging" of immigrant quotas imposed under the Displaced Persons Act of 1948 and other subsequent acts. It also provided for the granting of nonquota status to aliens qualifying under the first three preference groups on whose behalf petitions had been filed by a specified date.

The Refugee-Escapee Act of 1957 facilitated the admission into the United States of stepchildren, illegitimate children, and adopted children. It also conferred first preference status on the spouse and children of first preference immigrants if following to join the immigrant, set an age limit of 14 for the adoption of orphans to qualify for nonquota status, and further defined which orphans were eligible under the act. The Attorney General also received the authority, through the Refugee-Escapee Act of 1957, to admit aliens formerly excludable from the United States.

The Soviet invasion of Hungary in 1956 resulted in an acute refugee problem in central Europe and the desire on the part of many displaced persons to immigrate to — and settle in — the United States. To address this situation, the United States Congress passed, and President Eisenhower signed on July 25, 1958, a law which granted admission for permanent residence to Hungarian parolees of at least two years' residence in the United States, on condition that the alien was admissible at the time of entry and was still admissible.

This action was followed with an official act passed by the United States Congress, and signed into law by President Eisenhower on August 21, 1958. It authorized the Attorney General to adjust nonimmigrant aliens from temporary to permanent resident status subject to visa availability.

It has always been important for immigrants admitted to the United States to have their spouses and children also admitted as immigrants. In 1959, steps were taken to broadly liberalize the definition of admissible family members. The official act passed by the United States Congress, and signed into law by President Eisenhower on September 22, 1959, facilitated the entry of fiancees and relatives of alien residents and citizens of the United States by reclassifying certain categories of relatives into preference portions of the immigration quotas. This was designed to assist in reuniting families on a permanent basis, through the amendments to the Immigration and Nationality Act of 1952, and through temporary programs.

The last — and one of the most important — immigration laws enacted during the Eisenhower Administration was the Fair Share Refugee Act, which was signed into law by the President on July 14, 1960. This law authorized the Attorney General to parole up to 500 alien refugee-escapees and make them eligible for permanent residence, and amended the act of September 2, 1958 to extend it to June 30, 1962.

The Fair Share Refugee Act amended the act of September 11, 1957, which provided special nonquota immigrant visas for adopted or to-be-adopted orphans under 14 years of age, extending the act to June 30, 1961. The law also amended the Immigration and Nationality Act of 1952, adding possession of marijuana to the sections concerning excludable and deportable offenses, and it made alien seamen ineligible for adjustment from temporary to permanent resident status.

Between the years of 1951 and 1960, a total of 2,515,479 immigrants entered the United States. The largest nationality group was the 477,765 who arrived from Germany, followed by 377,952 who arrived from Canada, 299,811 who arrived from Mexico, and 202,824 who immigrated from the United Kingdom.

Above: President Dwight Eisenhower, whose administration would be the first to implement immigration policies against the backdrop of the historic Immigration and Nationality Act of 1952.

IMMIGRATION IN THE LATE TWENTIETH CENTURY

The years from 1960 through 1968 were years of substantial social and cultural changes in the United States. The years of the Kennedy and Johnson presidential administrations were years of change unprecedented — except for the Civil War years and World War II — in the history of the United States. These changes were, of course, reflected in United States public opinion regarding immigration and immigrants.

Former Democratic United States Senators John Fitzgerald Kennedy and Lyndon Baines Johnson were sworn in as President and Vice President of the United States on January 20, 1961. When Kennedy was assassinated on November 22, 1963, Johnson succeeded him, serving until January 20, 1969. Both Kennedy and Johnson were regarded — both at the time of their administrations and in hindsight — as "activist" presidents who advocated and signed a great deal of domestic social legislation. Examples include passage of the 1965 Voting Rights Act and the "War On Poverty." The Johnson years were marred by an increasing United

Opposite: The colorful and brightly illuminated dragon is the grand finale in the annual Chinese New Year's parade in San Francisco. The popular event attracts tens of thousands of spectators.

Below: Japanese and Chinese dining establishments side by side, an American street scene.

States involvement in the stalemate of the Vietnam War, the "Credibility Gap" in the public perception of the presidency and a mushrooming distrust of the United States government by the people of the United States. Actions to amend the Immigration and Nationality Act of 1952 stopped short of the general policy reform promoted by President Eisenhower. Eventually, the need for remedial legislation led Americans to realize that the national origins quota system no longer worked. The Immigration and Nationality Act of 1952 had become increasingly unpopular. In 1962, an amendment to the act tempered national origins with "humanitarian values" by creating a temporary program to allow nonquota status for certain backlogged preference cases.

During the early 1960s, the Kennedy Administration began a program of broad domestic reform. As part of this plan, President Kennedy, in 1963, sent a proposal to Congress to revise and update national immigration policy. He and other reformers opposed the national origins policy because it chose immigrants along racial and ethnic lines. By the early 1960s, many Americans had changed attitudes about racial and other forms of discrimination, and supported the movement for reform.

Meanwhile, the first official immigration act of the Kennedy years was passed by the United States Congress and signed into law by President Kennedy on September 26, 1961. This law liberalized the quota provisions of the Immigration and Nationality Act of 1952 by eliminating the ceiling of 2,000 on the aggregate quota of the Asia-Pacific triangle, codifying and making permanent the law for admission of adopted children, establishing a single statutory form of judicial review of orders of deportation, and insuring a minimum quota of 100 for newly independent nations — especially those in Africa. In keeping with the

Kennedy Administration's general dislike for race-based policies of all kinds, the new legislation called for the omission of information on race and ethnic origin from United States visa applications.

The 1961 law also provided that whenever one or more quota areas had a change of boundaries which might lessen their aggregate quota, they were to maintain the quotas they had before the change took place. The act strengthened the law against the fraudulent gaining of nonquota status by marriage, and it authorized the Public Health Service to determine which diseases were dangerous and contagious in constituting grounds for exclusion.

A further liberalization of United States immigration law occurred through the official act passed by the United States Congress and signed into law by President Kennedy on October 24, 1962. This law granted nonquota immigrant visas for certain aliens eligible for fourth preference (such as brothers, sisters, and children of citizens) and for aliens with special occupational skills. As a housekeeping measure, the 1962 law called for a semimonthly report to Congress from the Attorney General of first preference petitions approved, and it created a record of lawful entry and provided for suspension of deportation for aliens

who were physically present in the United States for at least seven years in some cases, and 10 years in others.

On October 3, 1965, President Johnson, in his first major immigration initiative, signed a series of important amendments to the Immigration and Nationality Act of 1952. Among the most significant of these was the provision which abolished the national origins quota system that dated back to the Immigration Act of 1924 (and was incorporated into the Immigration and Nationality Act of 1952). The 1965 provision thus eliminated national origin, race, or ancestry as a basis for immigration to the United States.

The law introduced a prerequisite for the issuance of a visa of an affirmative finding by the Secretary of Labor that an alien seeking to enter as a worker will not replace a worker in the United States nor adversely affect the wages and working conditions of similarly employed individuals in the United States.

The 1965 law also established two categories of immigrants not subject to numerical restrictions. These were immediate relatives (such as spouses, children, parents) of United States citizens, and "special immigrants." The latter were defined as "ministers of religion, certain former employees of the United States government abroad, certain persons who lost citizenship (by marriage or by service in foreign armed forces), and certain foreign medical graduates."

The Immigration and Nationality Act Amendments of 1965 also established allocation of immigrant visas on a first-come, first-served basis, subject to a seven-category preference system for relatives of United States citizens and permanent resident aliens (for the reunification of families) and for persons with special occupational skills, abilities, or training needed in the United States. The 1965 amendments set numerical limits to replace the quota system and gave preference, or priority, to family members of citizens or permanent residents. They also gave preference to immigrants with skills in demand in the United States. A preference was also established for conditional entrants, which included refugees. The new numerical limits took effect July 1, 1968. For the Eastern

Hemisphere the limit became 170,000, with no more than 20,000 immigrant visas to be issued to nationals from any single country. Between December 1, 1965 and July 1, 1968, a special immigrant pool was established to give unused quota numbers to persons from countries with backlogged quotas.

The Select Commission on Western Hemisphere Immigration recommended against setting numerical limits on Western Hemisphere immigration, but Congress did not take action on those recommendations. On July 1, 1968, the first numerical limit on immigration from the Western Hemisphere began and was set at 120,000 annually. Western Hemisphere immigration was strictly on a first-come, first-served basis. Neither country limits or preference categories were used.

Immigrants applying for skills-related visas first had to obtain certification from the Secretary of Labor that no United States workers were able, willing, or qualified to render such services. The Labor Secretary also decided if admitting such workers would be harmful to similar workers in the United States. Previously, immigrants admitted on the basis of their skills received visas and entered unless the Labor Department certified no need for their services.

These changes, and expanding international air travel, caused the Immigration and Naturalization Service to change many of its methods. For the task of inspection the Service relied more on "pre-clearance," and introduced border crossing cards for Mexican citizens. Also, after the United States instituted a one-stop land and two-stop airport inspection procedure, the Immigration and Naturalization Service cooperated more closely with other inspecting agencies, such as the Customs Service, Department of Agriculture, and Public Health Service.

Immigration and Naturalization Service enforcement officers began to face a rising number of illegal entries after 1966. The United States Border Patrol, created in 1924 to patrol the borders, had continued to grow and evolve, especially during World War II. The Patrol's war-related work included guarding diplomats and detention camps. After the war, the problem of illegal entry grew along the Mexican Border. In response, by 1950, a

Above: Border Patrol checkpoints, such as this one near San Clemente, California, are an important tool in stemming the tide of illegal immigration into the United States.

shift of stations and patrol agents to the southern border was under way. After the number of illegal aliens apprehended grew to more than 500,000 in 1952, the Immigration and Naturalization Service launched "Operation Wetback." This 1954 operation was described at the time as a Service-wide effort to sweep down, through California and Texas, and "drive" illegal aliens out of the country. Afterward, in 1955, an enlarged Border Patrol tried to hold the line at the southern border. Despite the Patrol's efforts, several factors caused the number of illegal entries to grow again in the 1960s. Termination of the Bracero Program in 1964, which for a generation had allowed temporary workers to cross the border legally, was one factor. Another, though less significant, was the first numerical limit put on Western Hemisphere immigration by the 1965 amendments.

The Freedom of Information Act, which was signed by President Johnson on July 4, 1966, was a milestone civil liberties law. Becoming effective on July 4, 1967, it was designed to make most government records — except those that were classified for reasons of national security — available to the general public. In terms of immigration records, the Freedom of Information Act provided that the record of every proceeding before the Immigration and Naturalization Service in an individual's case be made available to that person and/or his attorney of record. It also required that public reading rooms be established in each Central and District office of the Immigration and Naturalization Service, where copies of the Immigration and Naturalization Service decisions could be made available to the public.

The Western Hemisphere nation that occupied the attention of the Kennedy and Johnson administrations more than any other was Cuba. In 1959, the Communist revolutionary Fidel Castro had seized power in this island nation 90 miles from the United States. Castro's confiscation of private property and oppressive rule led large numbers of people from the middle and upper classes in Cuba to flee Cuba. Some of these persons immigrated to other Caribbean and Latin American nations, but many immigrated to the United States, particularly Florida, subject to then-existing immigration law.

By 1966, the waves of immigration from Cuba, and the status of Cuban refugees, necessitated specific United States legislation. The official act passed by the United States Congress and signed into law by President Johnson on November 2, 1966 authorized the Attorney General to adjust the status of Cuban refugees to that of permanent resident alien, chargeable to the 120,000 annual limit for the Western Hemisphere.

By the 1960s, changes in transportation technology, especially jetliners, made people of all over the world much more mobile. World civilization was becoming, in the phrase coined by 1960s social philosopher Marshall McLuhan, a "global village." It had once been rare to find people living and working in foreign countries without having actually immigrated to those countries. By the 1960s, however, it had become — and would remain — common for Americans to be living and working abroad. As might have been expected, United States citizens living and working abroad had children who were born in foreign countries. Because it was considered desirable for these children to have United States citizenship, Congress passed a law which was signed by

President Johnson on November 6, 1966 that extended derivative citizenship to children born on or after December 24, 1952 of civilian United States citizens serving abroad. The law also provided that time spent abroad by United States citizens (or their dependent children) in the employ of the United States government or certain international organizations could be treated as physical presence in the United States for the purpose of transmitting United States citizenship to children born abroad.

The United States citizenship theme was continued in the official act passed by the United States Congress, and signed into law by President Johnson on December 18, 1967, that facilitated the expeditious naturalization of certain noncitizen employees of United States nonprofit organizations.

Although he never intended it to be the centerpiece of his legacy, Lyndon Johnson's presidency will forever be associated with the Vietnam War. The last year of his presidency began with the Tet Offensive of February 1968, which demonstrated that the United States would be unable to win the Vietnam War without an investment of personnel and strategic

Above: Looking north across the international bridge over the Rio Grande that connects El Paso, Texas and Ciudad Juarez, Mexico, circa 1981. The United States port of entry and immigration station is visible at the bottom of the bridge in the center of this picture.

Below: A line of non-United States citizens and would-be immigrants await processing at a border station, circa 1970.

commitment that the people of the United States were unwilling to allow Johnson to make. Against the backdrop of sinking American morale about the war, and dissatisfaction with Johnson's presidency, Johnson announced that he would not run for a second term and he spent the rest of his term making desperate and ineffective attempts to withdraw the United States from the war.

With the above in mind, it is interesting to note that the last immigration legislation to pass through Congress during the Johnson administration dealt with Vietnam. Signed into law by President Johnson on October 24, 1968, this law was designed to reward foreign nationals — especially South Vietnamese citizens — who had helped the United States war effort in Vietnam and who wanted to live in the United States. It amended the Immigration and Nationality Act of 1952, providing for expeditious naturalization of noncitizens — especially Vietnamese — who had "rendered honorable services in the United States armed forces during the Vietnam conflict, or in other periods of military hostilities."

Between the years of 1961 and 1970, however, immigration from Asia was insignificant compared to what it would become in later decades. There were 98,376 immigrants from the Philippines and 75,007 from Hong Kong, but only 4,340 from Vietnam. Meanwhile,

immigration from Western Hemisphere nations accounted for a sizable proportion of the total of 3,321,677 immigrants who entered the United States. The largest nationality group was the 453,937 who arrived from Mexico, followed by 413,310 who arrived from Canada. The Western Hemisphere numbers were also augmented by the 208,536 people who fled Fidel Castro's takeover of Cuba. Meanwhile, European immigration continued to be important, with 214,111 immigrants coming from Italy, 213,822 from the United Kingdom and 190,796 from Germany.

The Nixon-Ford Administrations

While the Republican Party affiliations of Presidents Richard Nixon and Gerald Ford associate them with conservative policies, the records of their administrations tend to show them as being as liberal on immigration issues as Presidents Kennedy and Johnson. Though widely discredited for his part in the 1972 Watergate Scandal that led to his resignation in disgrace on August 9, 1974, President Richard Milhous Nixon was elected to the presidency twice and enjoyed great popularity through much of his tenure. Gerald Ford, on the other hand, was a highly regarded congressional leader who is remembered as the only United States president never to win a national election. Ford was appointed as Vice President when Spiro Agnew, Nixon's elected Vice President, resigned. He assumed the presidency upon Nixon's resignation in 1974, served out Nixon's term, and failed to win the 1976 election in his own right, so the two presidencies are linked as a single administrative era.

The first immigration legislation passed during the Nixon Administration was a liberalization law signed by President Nixon on April 7, 1970. This law created two new classes of nonimmigrant admission — fiancees of United States citizens and intracompany transferees. It also modified the temporary worker class of nonimmigrant admission, especially in regard to workers of distinguished merit and ability. Furthermore, this law altered the provisions of the law regarding the two-year residence requirement, making it easier for nonimmigrants who were in the United States as exchange visitors to adjust to a different nonimmigrant status or to permanent resident status.

The official act passed by the United States Congress and signed into law by Presi-

dent Nixon on August 10, 1971 amended the Communications Act of 1934, providing that lawful permanent resident aliens be permitted to operate amateur radio stations in the United States and hold licenses for their stations.

The Nixon Administration also inherited the Vietnam War, which had begun during the Johnson Administration and, despite promises to the contrary, continued to pursue it at increased levels of personnel and material commitment. One important — and notorious — aspect of the Vietnam Era was the drafting of male United States citizens under the Selective Service Act. The military draft and the Selective Service Act were extremely unpopular, especially with men between the ages of 18 and 26.

Also unpopular — especially among those who were ineligible — was the system of deferments that were available to certain people. One of the more controversial pieces of Nixon Administration legislation having to do with immigration also dealt with draft deferments. Passed by the United States Congress, and signed into law by President Nixon on September 28, 1971, this law amended the Selective Service Act of 1967 so that registration for the Selective Service would *not* be applicable to any alien admitted to the United States as a nonimmigrant, as long as he continued to maintain a lawful nonimmigrant status in the United States. This law further stated that "No alien residing in the United States for less than one year would be inducted for training and service into the United States armed forces."

Ironically, the last two immigration laws enacted during the presidency of Richard Nixon were extremely liberal laws signed immediately at the time that the Watergate Scandal was just coming to light. The official act passed by the United States Congress, and signed into law by President Nixon on October 27, 1972, reduced restrictions concerning residence requirements for retention of United States citizenship acquired by birth abroad through a United States citizen parent and an alien parent. The Social Security Act Amendments signed on October 30, 1972 provided that Social Security numbers be assigned to aliens at the time of their lawful admission to the United States for permanent residence or temporarily to engage in lawful employment.

In terms of immigration, the legislative history of the brief Ford Administration was actually more extensive than that of Ford's predecessor. Initially, the Ford Administration

dealt with the large influx of refugees that were coming into the United States from Asia, especially Indochina. The first of these immigration laws — signed by President Ford on October 20, 1974 — repealed the "Coolie Trade" legislation of 1862. Such legislation, passed to protect Chinese and Japanese aliens from exploitation that was caused by discriminatory treatment from immigration laws then in effect, had become virtually inoperative because most of the laws singling out Asian peoples had been repealed or modified.

Just as Vietnam had dominated much of the history of the Johnson and Nixon Administrations, the single most important foreign policy event of Gerald Ford's presidency was the capture and dissolution of South Viet-

Above: A pedestrian crossing point on the Mexico-United States border. Security is tight although the bridge toll is low. The toll is for the use of a bridge, not the price of crossing the border.

nam by North Vietnam, which occurred on April 30, 1975 after a war that had lasted 21 years and had involved the United States for more than a decade. President Ford's response to this included the Indochina Migration and Refugee Assistance Act of May 23, 1975, which established a program of domestic resettlement assistance for refugees and immigrants who had fled from Cambodia and South Vietnam as those two countries were swallowed by invading armies.

Immigration and Naturalization Service enforcement officers had begun to face a rising number of illegal entries after 1966 as a result of the termination of the Bracero Program in 1964 and the numerical limitation put on Western Hemisphere immigration by the 1965 amendments. The United States Border Patrol, created in 1924, faced an even more complex situation in the 1970s, when the business of alien smuggling began to involve drug smuggling as well.

The House of Representatives' Committee on the Judiciary held hearings on illegal immigration in 1971 and 1972. In 1975, President Ford established a Domestic Council Committee on Illegal Aliens to study and report on the subject. These activities served to

increase congressional, executive, and public interest in illegal immigration.

The Immigration and Naturalization Service and its Border Patrol reacted to the border situation in several ways. Again, manpower grew and shifted to problem areas. Use of electronic surveillance equipment increased from the early 1970s.

An act passed by the United States Congress and signed into law by President Ford on June 21, 1976 made Laotians eligible for programs established by the Indochina Migration and Refugee Assistance Act of 1975.

Compared to the Indochina Migration and Refugee Assistance Act of 1975, the law signed by President Ford on October 12, 1976 dealt with an extremely small category of immigrants. This law, actually the first *restrictive* immigration law in many, many years, placed restrictions on foreign medical school graduates — including both immigrants and nonimmigrants — coming to the United States for practice or training in the medical profession after January 10, 1977. However, just eight days later, President Ford signed another law which *eased* these same restrictions on foreign medical school graduates, effective on January 1, 1978. The second law specifically

exempted aliens who were "of national or international renown in the field of medicine." It also exempted certain alien physicians already in the United States from the examination requirement.

The latter law contained another, somewhat restrictive — albeit logical — provision, which denied unemployment compensation to aliens not lawfully admitted for permanent residence or otherwise permanently residing in the United States.

Possibly the most far-reaching immigration legislation of the Ford Administration was the amendments to the Immigration and Nationality Act of 1952, which were passed by Congress and signed into law by President Ford on October 20, 1976. These applied the same 20,000 person-per-country limit to the Western Hemisphere as had been applied to the Eastern Hemisphere, and slightly modified the seven-category preference system and applied it to the Western Hemisphere.

The Immigration and Nationality Act Amendments of 1976 also changed the 1966 act that had given Cuban refugees permanent resident alien status, chargeable to the 120,000 annual limit for the Western Hemisphere. The 1976 amendments provided that Cuban refugees who were adjusted to permanent resident status would not be charged to any numerical limitation, provided they were physically present in the United States on or before the effective date of the amendments.

Liberalizations During the Carter Era

The 1976 election of James Earl "Jimmy" Carter as President of the United States was seen at the time as a repudiation of the scandal-plagued Nixon and Ford Administrations. Carter was also destined to be the most socially liberal President in a generation, and possibly the most socially liberal President in United States history.

The immigration policies of the Carter Administration were clearly liberal in character, and the Carter-era immigration laws were more extensive than those passed in any previous single-term presidency. The first of these dealt with the aftermath of the Vietnam War. Passed by the United States Congress, and

Above: A Latin American travel agency in a California city. Immigrants to the United States obviously wish to maintain ties to friends and relatives in "the old country" through frequent visits.

signed into law by President Carter on October 28, 1977, it permitted the adjustment to permanent resident status for Indochinese refugees who were natives or citizens of Vietnam, Laos, or Cambodia, and who were physically present in the United States for at least two years. This law also extended the time limit during which refugee assistance would be provided to such people.

An official act passed by the United States Congress, and signed into law by President Carter on October 5, 1978, combined the separate ceilings for Eastern and Western Hemisphere immigration into one single, worldwide limit of 290,000.

As had been the case in the wake of previous wars involving the United States, there was a move by many United States citizens to adopt orphaned or refugee children who were natives of the regions where the war had occurred. Such was the case with Southeast Asia, and immigration legislation was required. The act passed by the United States Congress, and signed into law by President Carter on October 5, 1978, made several changes pertaining to the adoption of alien children, including permission for United States citizens to petition for the classification of more than two alien orphans as immediate relatives.

Almost as a footnote, this law undertook a dramatic liberalization which eliminated the requirement of continuous residence in the United States for two years prior to filing for naturalization.

A further dramatic liberalization came two days later with the law passed by the United States Congress, and signed by President Carter on October 7, 1978. It had long been the policy of the United States to prohibit United States passport-holders from travelling to certain countries — such as North Korea, Cuba, and East Germany — with whom the United States did not have diplomatic relations. The October 7 act lifted these restrictions, and called for unrestricted use of passports to and in any country other than a country with which the United States was at war, where armed hostilities were in progress, or where there was imminent danger to the public health or the physical safety of United States travelers. In doing this, the law also made permanent the President's authority to regulate the entry of aliens and to require United States citizens to bear valid passports when entering or leaving the United States.

The October 7, 1978 law also declared it to be the general policy of the United States to impose restrictions on travel within the United States by citizens of another country

only when the government of that country imposes restrictions on travel of United States citizens within that country.

Over the course of the next three weeks, the Democratic Congress and the Carter Administration created many other changes in United States immigration policy. The official act passed by Congress and signed into law by President Carter on October 14, 1978 required any alien who acquired or transferred any interest in agricultural land to submit a report to the Secretary of Agriculture within 90 days after acquisition or transfer.

The act passed by Congress and signed into law by President Carter on October 30, 1978 was written specifically to deal with alleged former Nazis who were suspected of war crimes and were living in the United States. The law provided for the exclusion and expulsion of aliens who persecuted others on the basis of race, religion, national origin, or political opinion under the direction of the Nazi government of Germany or its allies.

By the late 1970s, the illicit business of smuggling aliens in to the United States — which had always existed — had emerged as a serious problem for United States Border Patrol officers and other Immigration and Naturalization Service officials. This issue was addressed by the act passed by the United States Congress and signed into law by President Carter on November 2, 1978, which provided for the seizure and forfeiture of vessels, vehicles, and aircraft used in smuggling aliens or knowingly transporting aliens to the United States illegally. An exception was made where the owner or person in control did not consent to the illegal act.

Perhaps the most controversial foreign policy initiative of the Carter Administration was to turn the United States-built and United States government-owned Panama Canal over to the Republic of Panama. The Panama Canal Zone, a United States Territory, was abandoned under the Panama Canal Act of 1979, signed by President Carter on September 27. Its immi-

gration policy provisions included allowing the admission of aliens who had been employed on or before 1977 with the Panama Canal Company, the Canal Zone government, or the United States government in the Canal Zone — as well as their families — into the United States as permanent residents.

By the late twentieth century, immigrants to the United States no longer came from the same sources that immigrants had in the past. The sources of immigration had shifted after World War II, when American interests and influence turned to other parts of the world. As in earlier eras of American history,

Below: The Spanish language is quite common in the signage of areas that boast a large Latin American immigrant population.

war and economic crises pushed people away from their homes while economic opportunity drew them to the United States.

An earlier shift in the source of immigration occurred near the turn of the century. Throughout most of the nineteenth century, most immigrants came from northern and Western Europe. The first shift came around 1890, when more immigrants came from southern and eastern Europe. Until about 1965 most immigrants still came from Europe. Only about five percent came from Asia.

The 1965 amendments of the Immigration and Nationality Act, which eliminated the national origins system, began another shift. Under the 1965 amendments more

immigrants were permitted to come from Asia. Also, refugees from Cuba in 1960 marked a change in the source of refugees. Rather than from Europe, refugees increasingly came from Asia, especially Laos, Cambodia, and Vietnam. Later, in the 1980s, refugees began to come from Central America as well.

As the history of American immigration policy shows, the United States reacted to waves of refugees as they arose, rather than through a coherent policy. The Attorney General frequently used his power to parole groups of aliens into the country in response to specific issues or events, or as a way to protect the public interest. Initially, a group of refugees, such as Cuban refugees, were paroled into the country. Later, Congress would pass special legislation allowing individuals of that group to adjust from refugee to immigrant status. The Immigration and Naturalization Service administered a special program for Indochinese refugees in the 1970s. In this case, handling so many entries in so little time forced the Immigration and Naturalization Service to set up special temporary offices. The need for a better policy to respond to refugee crises later led to passage of the Refugee Act in 1980. One of the truly important immigration laws enacted during the Carter Administration, it was signed by President Carter on March 17 of that year.

The Refugee Act of 1980 provided the first permanent and systematic procedure for the admission and effective resettlement of refugees of special humanitarian concern to the United States. In so doing, the law eliminated refugees as a category of the preference system and set the worldwide ceiling of immigration to the United States at 270,000 annually — exclusive of refugees. The Refugee Act of 1980 also established procedures for annual consultation with Congress on numbers and allocations of refugees to be admitted in each fiscal year, as well as procedures for responding to emergency refugee situations. The Refugee Act of 1980 was, in turn, used to establish a comprehensive program for domestic resettlement of refugees, and it also provided for adjustment to permanent resident status of refugees who had been physically present in the United States for at least one year and of asylees one year after asylum was granted.

Finally, the Refugee Act of 1980 defined the term "refugee" to conform to the 1967 United Nations Protocol on Refugees,

and it made clear the distinction between refugee and asylee status.

The final immigration initiative undertaken by the Carter Administration — passed less than a month before an election that it was predicted to lose — was the Refugee Education Assistance Act of 1980. Passed by the Democrat-controlled Congress and signed by President Carter on October 10, the Refugee Education Assistance Act of 1980 was typical of Carter Administration legislation which allocated enormous increases in monetary outlays for a vast array of social programs, many of which had never previously existed. In this case, a program of formula grants to state education agencies was established for the basic education of refugee children. Also provided were services to Cuban and Haitian entrants that were identical to those which had previously been provided for refugees under the Refugee Act of 1980.

Between April 15, 1980 and October 20, 1980, because of a special invitation issued by President Carter, a large number of Cubans arrived from the Mariel Harbor in Cuba in what was known as the Mariel Boatlift.

These people, along with Haitians who entered the United States illegally before January 1, 1981 were subsequently accorded a dedicated "Cuban/Haitian Entrant Status." Cubans and Haitians meeting these criteria who had lived in the United States since before January 1, 1982, were allowed to adjust to permanent resident status under a provision of the Immigration Reform and Control Act.

The decade of 1971-1980 saw a major demographic shift in the origin of immigrants to the United States. Immigration from Mexico — which had begun to be a major factor in the totals during the 1950s — continued to increase in the 1970s. Meanwhile, with changes in the immigration laws and the end of the war in Southeast Asia in 1975, immigration from the Far East exceeded immigration from Europe for the first time in history.

Between the years of 1971 and 1980, a total of 4,493,314 immigrants entered the United States. The largest nationality group was the 640,294 who arrived from Mexico, followed by 354,987 who arrived from the Philip-

pines and 267,638 who arrived from Korea. Thanks in part to President Carter's liberal attitude toward immigration from Cuba, 264,863 immigrants fled the Castro regime to enter the United States. Immigration from Vietnam stood at 172,820 for the decade, ahead of immigration from the United Kingdom — the largest source of European immigration — which numbered 137,374.

The Reagan Years

Just as the Carter Administration came into office in 1976 as a reaction to the corruption of the Nixon Administration, it was voted out of office in 1980 by voters displeased with what was perceived at the time as reckless spending and a mismanagement of the economy that had resulted in dangerously spiraling,

Above: Cities with a large Asian population often accommodate immigrants by posting street lines in a non-Roman alphabet. In this case, the language, alphabet and neighborhood are Chinese.

double-digit inflation. Former California Governor Ronald Reagan defeated Jimmy Carter on a platform that included cuts in spending on various federal programs.

Among the early spending cuts undertaken by the Reagan Administration were immigration-related programs that had been enacted by Reagan's predecessor. The Supplemental Appropriations and Rescissions Act passed by the United States Congress, and signed into law by President Reagan on June 5, 1981, reduced the previously-appropriated funds for migration and refugee assistance, including funds provided for the reception and processing of Cuban and Haitian entrants.

The federal appropriations bill for fiscal year 1982, passed by Congress and signed into law by President Reagan on August 13, 1981, also contained items restricting the access of aliens to various publicly-funded benefits. Among the immigration-related provisions was the preclusion of the Secretary of Housing and Urban Development from making financial assistance available to any alien unless that alien was a resident of the United States by virtue of admission or adjustment as a permanent resident alien, refugee or asylee, parolee, conditional entrant, or pursuant to withholding of deportation. Alien visitors, tourists, diplomats, and students were specifically excluded.

The federal appropriations bill for fiscal year 1982 also restricted the eligibility of noncitizens to the Aid to Families with Dependent Children program, which was originally intended for United States citizens. However, the act passed by Congress and signed into law by President Reagan on September 30, 1982 allowed admission as permanent residents to certain nonimmigrant aliens residing in the Virgin Islands.

In turn, the act passed by Congress, and signed into law by President Reagan on October 2, 1982, greatly limited the categories of aliens to whom the Legal Services Corporation might provide legal assistance.

By the mid-1980s, the issue of Amerasian children — illegitimate children fathered by United States servicemen in Southeast Asia — had come to the fore. These children, who were still living in Southeast Asia with their Asian mothers, were now reaching their late teens and early twenties and many were demanding entry into the United States. To address this growing problem Congress passed and President Reagan signed on October 22, 1982, a law which provided that children born of United States citizen fathers in Korea, Vietnam, Laos, Cambodia (then known as Kampuchea), or Thailand after 1950 and before enactment, could come to the United States as

immediate relatives or as first or fourth preference immigrants.

Over the next several years, the Amerasian teenagers and young adults flooded into the United States to begin new lives, but faced problems, such as rejection by their United States-citizen fathers and a language barrier. To aid the Amerasians and to facilitate their arrival and settlement, Congress passed the Amerasian Homecoming Act of 1987, which was signed into law by President Reagan on December 22 of that year. Essentially, it was an appropriations law providing for admission of children born in Vietnam between specified dates to Vietnamese mothers and American fathers, together with their immediate relatives. They were to be admitted as nonquota immigrants but to receive refugee program benefits.

As had occurred during the Kennedy, Johnson, and Ford Administrations, the Reagan Administration enacted a series of amendments to the Immigration and Nationality Act of 1952. Known as the Immigration and Naturalization Service Efficiency Act of 1981, these amendments changed not only the Immigration and Nationality Act of 1952, but the Immigration Act of November 2, 1978.

Passed by Congress and signed into law by President Reagan on December 20, 1981, the Immigration and Naturalization Service Efficiency Act authorized the Immigration and Naturalization Service to seize vehicles without having to establish whether the owner was involved in the illegal activity in question, and it eliminated the requirement that the government bear administrative and incidental expenses where an innocent owner is involved.

The new law also eliminated the requirement that the Immigration and Naturalization Service satisfy any valid lien or other third party interest in a vehicle without expense to the interest holder, and it eliminated the required annual notification by aliens of their current address.

Probably the most important immigration legislation that was passed during the eight years of the Reagan Administration was the Immigration Reform and Control Act of 1986 (IRCA), which was passed by Congress and signed into law by President Reagan on November 6, 1986. During the 1970s and through the mid-1980's, undocumented aliens and refugees had increasingly dominated the immigration issues before Congress.

Most illegal aliens came from countries neighboring the United States. Poor economic conditions in many developing and underdeveloped countries, especially in Mexico and Central America, pushed people

Above: This Hispanic market, like the Asian market on the opposite page, caters to an immigrant community that is shopping for familiar ingredients from back home.

away from their native lands. The prospect of employment at United States wages and the lack of means to enter legally induced many of these persons to enter the United States illegally. The economic imbalance between the United States and a migrant's home country was and is a major reason behind illegal migration. Family reunification and social and political unrest also create illegal alien flows.

Illegal immigration grew steadily each year. By the mid-1980s many Americans felt the United States had lost control of its borders. To many citizens, the social and economic costs of illegal immigration seemed too heavy a burden for the United States' economy to bear.

In 1979 the Select Commission on Immigration and Refugee Policy was established to study immigration issues and report to the President and Congress. Before reporting in March 1981, the Commission and its staff conducted extensive research, including public hearings and site visits, on the impact of immigration on American society. The Commission

recommended treating the issues of legal immigration and illegal immigration separately. In doing so, it formed the basis of debate for the next five years. During the first half of the 1980s, Congressional debate focused on control of illegal immigration. Following years of near-passage of reform legislation, Congress passed the Immigration Reform and Control Act in late 1986.

The Immigration Reform and Control Act of 1986 banned employing or recruiting workers who were ineligible to work in the United States. It also required employers to verify the employment eligibility of all workers hired. Violations by employers were punishable by employer sanctions, a series of fines which could range as high as $10,000. The act also contained a provision to prevent discrimination against citizens and legal aliens that might occur in hiring.

The Immigration Reform and Control Act of 1986 is recalled as a comprehensive immigration law which accomplished a number of important goals. It authorized temporary —

and later permanent — resident status for aliens who had resided in the United States in an unlawful status since January 1, 1982. This amnesty act pertained to those who had entered the United States illegally or as temporary visitors with an authorized stay expiring before that date (or with the government's knowledge of their unlawful status before that date).

This act also provided the Special Agricultural Worker (SAW) Program, which granted temporary, and later permanent, status to former illegal aliens who worked at least 90 days in seasonal agriculture during the year ending May 1, 1986.

In addition to its generous and lenient amnesty, the Immigration Reform and Control Act of 1986 created sanctions prohibiting employers from knowingly hiring, recruiting, or referring for a fee aliens not authorized to work in the United States, it increased enforcement at United States borders; created a new classification of seasonal agricultural worker; and contained provisions for the legalization of certain of these workers.

The Immigration Reform and Control Act of 1986 also changed the "registry date," or the date from which an alien could have resided illegally and continuously in the United States and yet still qualify for adjustment to permanent resident status. This date was extended from June 30, 1948 to January 1, 1972.

The new law also authorized adjustment to permanent resident status for Cubans and Haitians who had entered the United States without inspection and who had continuously resided in the United States since January 1, 1982. It increased the numerical limitation for immigrants admitted under the preference system for dependent areas from 600 to 5,000 beginning in fiscal year 1988. It created a new special immigrant category for certain retired employees of international organizations and their families, and a new nonimmigrant status for parents and children of such immigrants.

In terms of changes in visa requirements, the Immigration Reform and Control Act of 1986 created a nonimmigrant Visa Waiver Pilot Program allowing certain aliens

Above: A lively street scene on Waverly Place in San Francisco's Chinatown. This area has been a center of Chinese-American cultural activity for more than a century.

to visit the United States without applying for a nonimmigrant visa and it allocated 5,000 non-preference visas in each of fiscal years 1987 and 1988 for aliens born in countries from which immigration was adversely affected by the 1965 act.

Almost immediately after passage of the landmark Immigration Reform and Control Act of 1986, Congress passed the Immigration Marriage Fraud Amendments of 1989, which were signed by President Reagan on November 10, 1986. The Immigration Marriage Fraud Amendments stipulated that aliens deriving their immigrant status based on a marriage of less than two years were conditional immigrants. To remove conditional status, the alien had to apply within 90 days after his or her second-year anniversary of receiving conditional status. The Immigration Marriage Fraud Amendments also addressed the scam of mail order brides using a planned marriage as a ploy to enter the United States by requiring alien fiancees of United States citizens to have met their citizen petitioner — the person that

they were claiming that they intended to marry — in person within two years of the date the petition was filed.

Among the most significant — and most controversial — initiatives undertaken during the administrations of Ronald Reagan and George Bush were the notable United States-Canada Free Trade Agreement and the later North American Free Trade Agreement (NAFTA). As might be expected, there was accompanying immigration legislation. Passed by the United States Congress, and signed into law by President Reagan on September 28, 1988, the United States-Canada Free Trade Agreement Implementation Act facilitated temporary entry on a reciprocal basis between the United States and Canada, and established procedures for the temporary entry into the United States of Canadian citizen professional business persons to render services for remuneration. The United States-Canada Free Trade Agreement Implementation Act also provided that no nonimmigrant visa, prior petition, labor certifica-

tion, nor prior approval would be required for entry. However, appropriate documentation would have to be presented to the inspecting officer to establish Canadian citizenship (or in the reciprocal agreement, United States citizenship) and professional engagement in one of the occupations listed in the qualifying occupation schedule.

Thanks in part to the liberal laws enacted during the Carter Administration, the decade of the 1980s saw the largest number of immigrants entering the United States of any decade since the record total years of the 1901-1910 period.

Between the years of 1981 and 1990, a total of 7,338,062 immigrants entered the United States, with the totals for 1989 and 1990 exceeding one million for the first time since 1914. The 1,536,483 who entered in 1990 were the largest block of immigrants to enter the United States in its history, but the total would be topped a year later, when 1,877,167 people entered the United States in 1991.

The trend toward Latin American and Far East immigration continued, with 1,655,842 Mexicans being the largest nationality group to enter the United States during the 1980s, and the largest nationality group to enter the United States during any decade

since 2,045,877 Italians and 2,145,266 persons from the Austro-Hungarian Empire arrived in the record-setting first decade of the twentieth century.

Among other nationality groups, the overall total for Asia stood at 2,738,157 — compared to 761,550 for Europe — and included 548,764 Filipinos, 333,746 Koreans and 280,782 Vietnamese. In addition to those from Mexico, 1,802,444 persons arrived from Latin America and the Caribbean. These included 252,035 Dominicans and 213,539 persons from El Salvador.

The Bush Administration and the Immigration Act of 1990

Having served for eight years as President Ronald Reagan's Vice President, George Bush was sworn in as the 41st President of the United States on January 20, 1989. Among the important immigration initiatives undertaken during the Bush Administration were the Foreign Operations Act, the Chinese Student Protection Act, and the Soviet Scientists Immigration Act. The Immigration Act of 1990 was destined to be the most important overhaul of immigration law in nearly four decades.

The Foreign Operations Act, passed by Congress and signed into law by President Bush on November 21, 1989, was an appropriations law that provided for adjustment to permanent resident status for Soviet and Indochinese nationals who were paroled into the United States between certain dates after denial of refugee status.

The next immigration law to be enacted by the Bush Administration was the Nursing Relief Act of 1989, passed by Congress and signed into law by the President on December 18, 1989. It provided for adjustment from temporary to permanent resident status — without regard to numerical limitation — of certain nonimmigrants who were employed in the United States as registered nurses for at least three years and met established certification standards. This law also established a new nonimmigrant category for the temporary admission of qualified registered nurses. The Nursing Relief Act of 1989 was related to the act passed by Congress and signed by President Ronald Reagan on November 15, 1988 that provided for the extension of stay for certain nonimmigrant nurses.

Immigration reform in the 1980s, which produced the Refugee Act of 1980 and

Above: Dancers practice their steps at a mustering point in advance of a Cinco de Mayo parade in California. Note that the float in the background carries both the American and Mexican flags.

the Immigration Reform and Control Act in 1986, continued with the Immigration Act of 1990, enacted November 29, 1990. The 1990 law totally revamped the immigrant selection system. It provided for increases in the number of available immigrant visas and revised the preference categories governing permanent, legal immigration. Under this law, immigrant visas are granted in three separate categories: family-sponsored, employment-based, and "diversity" immigrants. The last category, diversity, initially provides visas to immigrants from countries that were adversely affected by the Immigration Act Amendments of 1965, and later provides visas to certain aliens from countries with low volumes of immigration. The Immigration Act of 1990 also recodified and restructured the grounds for deportation.

The 1990 act modified various provisions regarding naturalization, and provided for naturalization of certain Filipino veterans of World War II. The new law also established an administrative procedure for naturalization. New citizens may now choose between the traditional court proceeding or the new administrative process.

The Immigration Act of 1990 increased total immigration under an overall flexible cap of 675,000 immigrants beginning in fiscal year 1995, preceded by a 700,000 level during fiscal years 1992 through 1994. The 675,000 level was intended to consist of 480,000 family-sponsored, 140,000 employment-based, and 55,000 so-called "diversity immigrants."

The Immigration Act of 1990 revised — for the first time in decades — all grounds for exclusion and deportation, significantly rewriting the political and ideological grounds for exclusion and deportation. For example, the act repealed the ban against the admission of Communists as nonimmigrants and limited the exclusion of aliens on foreign policy grounds.

The new law authorized the Attorney General to grant temporary protected status to undocumented alien nationals of designated countries, subject to armed conflict or natural disasters in those designated countries.

The Immigration Act of 1990 also revised and established new nonimmigrant admission categories. Specifically, it redefined the temporary worker category, and limited number of aliens who may be issued visas or otherwise provided nonimmigrant status under this category to 65,000 annually. It limited the number of temporary worker category aliens who could be issued visas or otherwise provided nonimmigrant status to 66,000 annually, and it created new temporary worker admission categories, some of which would have annual caps on the number of aliens who could be issued visas or otherwise provided nonimmigrant status.

The act revised and extended the Visa Waiver Pilot Program through fiscal year 1994, and revised naturalization authority and requirements. The latter changes included

(1) transferring the exclusive jurisdiction to naturalize aliens from the federal and state courts to the Attorney General's office, (2) amending the substantive requirements for naturalization (the state residency requirements were revised and reduced to three months), (3) adding another ground for waiving the English language requirement, and (4) lifting the permanent ban on naturalization for aliens who applied to be relieved from United States military service because of those who previously served in the armed forces of the country of the alien's nationality.

The Immigration Act of 1990 revised enforcement activities by broadening the definition of "aggravated felony," imposing new legal restrictions on aliens convicted of such crimes, revising criminal and deportation provisions, and recodifying the 32 grounds for exclusion into nine categories, as well as including revising and repealing some of the grounds (especially health grounds). The act revised the Employer Sanctions provisions of the Immigration Reform and Control Act of 1986, and authorized funds to increase United States Border Patrol personnel by 1,000.

The Armed Forces Immigration Adjustment Act of 1991, which was signed into law by President Bush on October 1, 1991, modified somewhat the provisions of the Immigration Act of November 29, 1990. Specifically, the Armed Forces Immigration Adjustment Act of 1991 granted special immigrant status to certain types of aliens who honorably served in the Armed Forces of the United States for at least 12 years. It also delayed until April 1, 1992 the implementation of provisions relating to certain nonimmigrant visas.

The Refugee Act of 1980, the Immigration Reform and Control Act of 1986, and the Immigration Act of 1990 overhauled American immigration policy. They addressed United States policy toward refugees, control over illegal immigration, criteria for selection of immigrants, and exclusion and deportation of ineligible aliens. Like reforms of the past, they represent the United States' continuing effort to resolve the ongoing questions of immigration.

Signed into law by President Bush on December 12, 1991, the Miscellaneous and Technical Immigration and Naturalization Amendments Act amended certain elements of the Immigration Act of 1990. Among these changes, it revised provisions regarding the entrance of certain nonimmigrants, including the repeal of numerical limits of some visas.

In the wake of the 1989 crackdown on democracy advocates in the People's Republic of China, the United States undertook a vari-

Above: The Peace Pagoda in San Francisco's Japan Center.

ety of initiatives. On the immigration side, this included the Chinese Student Protection Act of 1992, which passed Congress and which was signed by President Bush on October 9, 1992. This law provided for adjustment to permanent resident status — as employment-based immigrants — those nationals of the People's Republic of China who had arrived in the United States after June 4, 1989 and before April 11, 1990.

One of the key immigration laws to be enacted as a result of the collapse of the Soviet Union was the Soviet Scientists Immigration Act of 1992. Signed into law by President Bush on October 10, 1992, this measure conferred permanent resident status — as employment-based immigrants — upon a maximum of 750 scientists from the independent states of the former Soviet Union and the Baltic states. The limit of 750 did not, however, include spouses and children of the Soviet scientists. The Soviet Scientists Immigration Act of 1992 stipulated that the scientists included must have held jobs in the biological, chemical, or nuclear technical fields or that they had worked in conjunction with a high technology defense project. However, the law waived the requirement that workers with expertise in these fields were needed by an employer in the United States.

The Clinton Years and Stricter Laws

The first member of the Democratic Party to occupy the White House in a dozen years, William Jefferson "Bill" Clinton was sworn in as President of the United States on January 20, 1993. His administration was to be defined by a much more conservative approach to most domestic policy issues than the administration of the previous Democratic President, James Earl "Jimmy" Carter, who had served from 1977 to 1981.

At the time that President Clinton took office, the controversial North American Free Trade Agreement (NAFTA) was working its way through the United States Congress. Angering some Democrats, Clinton sided with his Republican predecessors, Presidents Ronald Reagan and George Bush, to support NAFTA, which passed Congress and went to his desk for signature. Along with its accompanying immigration legislation, NAFTA was one of the important legislative milestones of the decade.

The North American Free Trade Agreement Implementation Act was signed into law by President Clinton on December 8, 1993, superseding the United States-Canada Free Trade Agreement Act of September 28, 1988. The new law would facilitate temporary entry on a reciprocal basis between the United States, Canada, and Mexico. It would also establish procedures for the temporary entry into the United States of Canadian and Mexican citizen professional business persons to render services for remuneration.

For Canadians, no nonimmigrant visa, prior petition, labor certification, or prior approval is required, but, as with the 1988 law, appropriate documentation must be presented to the inspecting officer establishing Canadian citizenship and professional engagement in one of the occupations listed in the qualifying occupation schedule. For Mexicans, however, the requirements are more strict. A nonimmigrant visa, prior petition by an employer, and Department of Labor attestation are required, in addition to proof of Mexican citizenship and professional engagement in one of the occupations listed in the qualifying occupation schedule.

For Canadians, under the North American Free Trade Agreement Implementation Act, nonimmigrant visas are not required of spouses and minor children who possess Canadian citizenship. However, for Mexicans, nonimmigrant visas are required of spouses and minor children who possess Mexican citizenship.

As for quantitative limitations under the North American Free Trade Agreement Implementation Act, there is no limit on Canadians, but Mexicans are limited to a number set — for a transition period for up to 10 years — at 5,500 initial approvals per year.

During the 1994-1996 period, the Clinton Administration enacted two of the toughest immigration reforms ever in response to international criminal activity and terrorism. The Violent Crime Control and Law Enforcement Act signed by President Clinton on September 13, 1994 authorized the establishment of a criminal alien tracking center, and established a new nonimmigrant classification for alien witness cooperation and for counter-terrorism information. It also revised deportation procedures for certain criminal aliens who are not permanent residents, and expanded special deportation proceedings. This law also provided and for expeditious deportation for denied asylum applicants, for improved border management through increased resources, and it strengthened penalties for passport and visa offenses.

The Anti-terrorism and Effective Death Penalty Act signed by President Clinton on April 24, 1996 expedited procedures for removal of alien terrorists and established specific measures to exclude members and representatives of terrorist organizations. These specific measures included providing for the exclusion of alien terrorists, waiving authority concerning notice of denial of application for visas, denying other forms of relief for alien terrorists, and finally, excluding from process any aliens who had not been inspected and admitted.

The 1996 law also modified asylum procedures to improve identification and the processing of alien terrorists. This included establishing mechanisms for denial of asylum to alien terrorists, granting authority to inspection officers to both inspect and exclude asylee applicants, and improving the judicial review process to expedite hearings and removal (if necessary) of alien terrorists.

Among the other provisions of the Anti-terrorism and Effective Death Penalty Act were that it provided access to certain confidential immigration and naturalization files through court order; it established a criminal alien identification system; it defined alien smuggling-related crimes as racketeer-influenced offenses; it granted authority for alien smuggling investigations; it expanded the criteria for deportation for crimes of moral turpitude and it established an interior repatriation program. The Anti-terrorism and Effective Death Penalty Act also allowed for the deportation of nonviolent offenders prior to their completion of a sentence of imprisonment; it authorized state and local law enforcement officials to arrest and detain certain illegal aliens; It expedited the process of criminal alien removal; it limited collateral attacks on underlying deportation orders, and it established deportation procedures for certain criminal aliens who were not permanent residents.

Above: The marquee of a Chinese-American theater.

Below: Ceremonial activity in San Francisco's Chinatown. As with many immigrant communities, Chinatown is a rich blend of both Western and traditional cultural elements.

The Immigration and Naturalization Service Today

The United States Immigration and Naturalization Service (INS) was created by the Act of March 3, 1891 and its purpose and responsibilities were further specified by the Immigration and Nationality Act, as amended (8 United States Code, 1101 note), which charges the Attorney General with the administration and enforcement of its provisions. The Immigration and Naturalization Service is headed by a commissioner, who reports to the Attorney General. The structure of the Immigration and Naturalization Service is divided into operational and management functions. Operations includes both Enforcement and Examinations programs. The management function covers information resources, finance, human resources, administration, and equal employment opportunity.

Overall policy and executive direction flow from the Washington, DC headquarters to 33 districts and 21 border patrol sectors throughout the United States. In addition, four regional offices provide administrative support to the field offices. The Immigration and Naturalization Service also maintains three district offices in Bangkok, Thailand, Mexico City, Mexico; and Rome, Italy.

Unique to the Service is the dual mission of providing information and service to the general public, while concurrently exercising its enforcement responsibilities. Its mission is divided into four major areas of responsibility: (1) facilitating the entry of persons legally admissible as visitors or as immigrants to the United States; (2) Granting benefits under the Immigration and Nationality Act, as amended, including providing assistance to those seeking permanent resident status or naturalization; (3) Preventing unlawful entry, employment, or receipt of benefits by those who are not entitled to them, and (4) Apprehending or removing those aliens who enter or remain illegally in the United States and/or whose stay is not in the public interest.

The Attorney General has delegated authority to the Commissioner of the Immigration and Naturalization Service to carry out a national immigration policy that will administer and enforce the immigration laws and promote the public health and safety, economic welfare, national security, and humanitarian interests of this country.

The operational and management functions of the Immigration and Naturaliza-

tion Service are organized among four executive divisions at Headquarters in Washington, DC. These are Programs, Field Operations, Policy and Planning, and Management. On the operational side, Programs oversees all enforcement and examinations functions and Field Operations provides executive direction to all field offices around the world.

Immigration and Naturalization Service operations are divided between two major program categories, Enforcement and Examinations. These categories reflect the traditional distinction between enforcing the requirements and administering the benefits of immigration law. The primary enforcement missions of the Immigration and Naturalization Service are to prevent aliens from entering the country illegally and to find and remove those who are living or working here illegally. These functions are performed by four enforcement programs, namely Border Patrol, Investigations, Intelligence, and Detention and Deportation. Investigation activities focus on enforcement of immigration laws within the interior of the United States. Plainclothes special agents use both traditional and innovative methods to investigate violations of immigration law and

aliens involved in criminal activities. Agents often participate in multi-agency task forces against narcotics trafficking, violent crime, document fraud, and traditional and nontraditional organized crime. They also try to identify incarcerated aliens who are deportable as a result of their criminal convictions. Agents monitor and inspect places of employment to apprehend unauthorized alien workers and to impose sanctions against employers who knowingly employ them. The Anti-Smuggling Branch of the Investigation Program is responsible for detecting, apprehending, and prosecuting sophisticated alien smuggling operations.

The Immigration and Naturalization Service intelligence teams collect, evaluate, analyze, and disseminate information relating to all Immigration and Naturalization Service missions, both Enforcement and Examinations. The Intelligence Program also directs the Headquarters Command Center, which maintains communications with other offices and agencies 24 hours a day.

The Detention and Deportation (D&D) Program is charged with taking criminals and illegal aliens into custody pending pro-

Above: While New York City has more Chinese residents than San Francisco, the latter city has the highest proportion of Chinese residents of any major city in the United States.

ceedings to determine either their status or their removal from the United States. D&D enforces the departure of these individuals as expeditiously as possible when they have exhausted all relief available to them under due process. D&D operates nine detention facilities, known as Service Processing Centers (SPCs) and places detainees, when necessary, in Bureau of Prisons institutions, approved contract facilities, or state and local jails.

The Immigration and Naturalization Service also works with other federal, state, and local law enforcement agencies in the national war on drugs. Since 1988, the Border Patrol has served as the primary agency for drug interdiction between the ports of entry, directly assisting other federal, state and local law enforcement agencies in preventing billions of dollars worth of illegal drugs from reaching United States markets.

At the same time, Immigration Inspectors work with their Customs Service counterparts to stop drug traffic at United States ports of entry. In the interior, Immigration and Naturalization Service special agents work with the multi-agency Organized Crime Drug Enforcement Task Force to investigate and dismantle large-scale operations in narcotics trafficking, arresting thousands of crimi-

nal aliens and seizing large amounts of narcotics, firearms, vehicles, cash, and other assets owned or used by the traffickers.

The Examinations Group at the Immigration and Naturalization Service includes Adjudication and Nationality, Inspections, Service Center Operations, and Administrative Appeals. These programs deal directly with foreign nationals who want to come to the United States temporarily or permanently and with resident aliens who want to become American citizens.

The Inspections group is responsible for screening all travelers arriving in the United States by air, land, or sea through some 250 ports of entry. This screening includes the examination and verification of travel documents for every alien seeking to enter the country. Last year, some 484 million travelers passed through immigration inspection.

The Adjudications and Nationality group receives and examines a variety of applications for immigration benefits, including petitions for citizenship. The Service Center Operations group oversees the work of Immigration Examiners and processing systems in four Service Centers, where most applications and petitions are adjudicated. These facilities are located in St. Albans, Vermont; Lincoln,

Nebraska; Dallas, Texas; and Laguna Niguel, California. In 1995 alone, the Immigration and Naturalization Service admitted about 716,000 new immigrants and 18 million nonimmigrants, such as tourists, students, business persons, diplomatic officials, and temporary workers. In addition, the Immigration and Naturalization Service naturalized 500,000 new citizens, welcomed more than 100,000 refugees, and granted asylum to more than 12,700 aliens who had fled persecution in their homelands.

The Responsibility Acts

In the history of immigration legislation, many of the individual presidential administrations are remembered for a particular milestone law. Theodore Roosevelt will be remembered for the Immigration Act of 1907, Woodrow Wilson will be remembered for the Immigration Act of 1917, Harry Truman will be remembered for the Immigration and Nationality Act of 1952, George Bush will be remembered for the Immigration Act of 1990, and Bill Clinton will be remembered for the far-reaching Personal Responsibility and Work Opportunity Reconciliation Act of 1996 and the com-

panion Illegal Immigration Reform and Immigrant Responsibility Act of 1996.

Passed by the United States Congress, the Personal Responsibility and Work Opportunity Reconciliation Act was signed by President Clinton on August 22, 1996. This law established restrictions on the eligibility of legal immigrants for means-tested public assistance, barred legal immigrants (with certain exceptions) from obtaining food stamps and Supplemental Security Income (SSI), and it established screening procedures for persons who were at that time current recipients of the food stamp and SSI programs.

The law also barred most legal immigrants — who entered the United States after the date of enactment — from most federal means-tested programs for five years. Under the law, the United States federal government provided the states with broad flexibility in setting public benefit eligibility rules for legal immigrants by allowing those states to bar current legal immigrants from both major federal programs and state programs.

The complex Personal Responsibility and Work Opportunity Reconciliation Act increased the responsibility of the immigrants'

Above: Cuban immigrant Margarita Uria Sanchez waves as she boards a plane which will take her and other Cubans from US Naval Station Guantanamo Bay, Cuba, to Homestead AFB, Florida, on January 31, 1996. She was the last to leave the immigrant processing center at Guantanamo Bay that was established on May 18, 1994, to provide humanitarian assistance to Haitians escaping political strife. A wave of Cuban migrants followed in August of that same year.

sponsors by making the affidavit of support legally enforceable, by imposing new requirements on sponsors, and by expanding sponsor-deeming requirements to more programs and lengthening the deeming period. The law also barred illegal, or "not qualified aliens," from most federal, state, and local public benefits, and required the Immigration and Naturalization Service to verify immigration status in order for aliens to receive most federal public benefits.

Passed by the United States Congress and sent to the White House just a month after the Personal Responsibility and Work Opportunity Reconciliation Act, the Illegal Immigration Reform and Immigrant Responsibility Act was signed into law by President Clinton on September 30, 1996. It established measures to control United States borders, protect legal workers through worksite enforcement, and remove criminal and other deportable aliens.

Specifically, the Illegal Immigration Reform and Immigrant Responsibility Act increased United States Border Patrol personnel, equipment, and technology, as well as enforcement personnel, at land and air ports of entry. The law also authorized improvements in barriers along the southwest border between

California and Texas, increased anti-smuggling authority and penalties for alien smuggling, and increased penalties for illegal entry, passport, and visa fraud, and for failure to depart.

The Illegal Immigration Reform and Immigrant Responsibility Act increased the Immigration and Naturalization Service investigators for worksite enforcement, alien smuggling, and "visa overstayers."

It established three voluntary pilot programs to confirm the employment eligibility of workers, and reduced the number and types of documents that may be presented to employers for identity and eligibility to work. The law broadly reformed exclusion and deportation procedures. Among these were such elements as the consolidation into a single removal process, as well as the institution of expedited removal to speed deportation and alien exclusion through more stringent grounds of admissibility.

As practical measures, the Illegal Immigration Reform and Immigrant Responsibility Act increased detention space for criminal and other deportable aliens, and instituted three-year and 10-year bars to admissibility for aliens seeking to reenter after having been unlawfully present in the United States, while barring the re-entry of individuals who

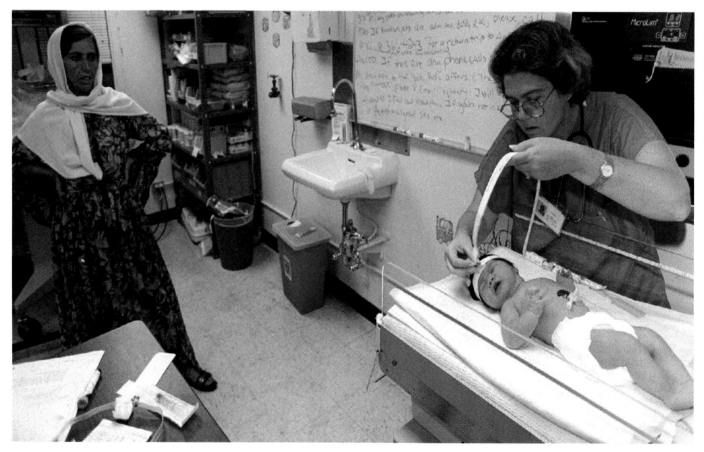

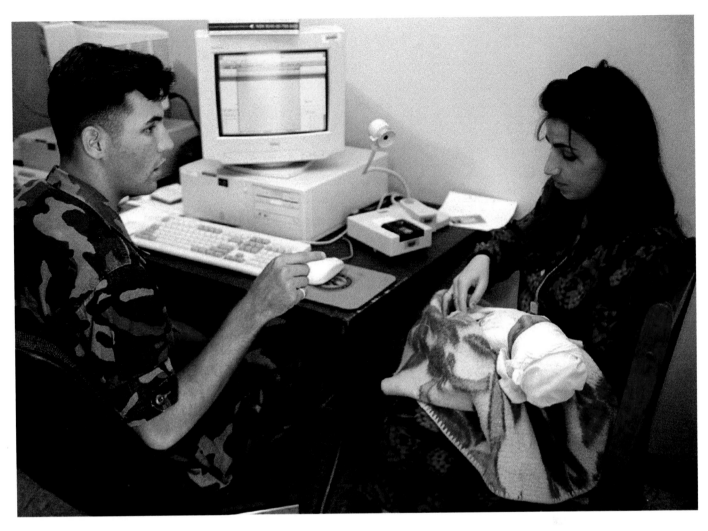

renounced their United States citizenship in order to avoid United States tax obligations.

On the "responsibility" side, the Illegal Immigration Reform and Immigrant Responsibility Act placed added restrictions on benefits that had been made available to aliens free of charge or at minimal cost. Among these measures were providing for a pilot program on limiting issuance of driver's licenses to illegal aliens; declaring illegal aliens ineligible for Social Security benefits; establishing procedures for requiring proof of citizenship for federal public benefits; establishing limitations on eligibility for preferential treatment of aliens not lawfully present on the basis of residence for higher education benefits and providing for verification of immigration status for purposes of Social Security and higher educational assistance.

The act also succeeded in tightening the requirement for an affidavit of support for sponsored immigrants and making this affidavit a legally binding contract to provide financial support; providing authority of states and political subdivisions of states to limit assistance to aliens in providing general cash public assistance and increasing the maximum criminal penalties for forging or counterfeiting the seal of a federal department or agency to facilitate benefit fraud by an unlawful alien.

Finally, the Illegal Immigration Reform and Immigrant Responsibility Act of 1996 recodified existing Immigration and Naturalization Service regulations regarding asylum; provided that the Attorney General's parole authority could be exercised only on a case-by-case basis for urgent humanitarian reasons or significant public health, and created new limits on the ability of students to attend public schools without reimbursing those institutions. The law also established new mandates for educational institutions to collect information on foreign students' status and nationality and provide it to the Immigration and Naturalization Service, tightened restrictions regarding foreign physicians' ability to work in the United States, and added new consular processing provisions while revising the visa waiver program.

Above: US Army Specialist Brandon Files interviews a Kurdish woman as he creates identification cards for her and her child at Andersen AFB on Guam during Operation Pacific Haven on September 27, 1996. Evacuees from Northern Iraq were sheltered and fed at the base and processed on a case-by-case basis for entry into the continental United States as quickly as possible.

Right: Parades in celebration of ethnic heritage have always been very important to immigrant communities in the United States, and to the descendants of immigrants. Since they first arrived in the United States, Irish immigrants have always gone out of their way to celebrate the feast day of the Emerald Isle's patron saint. St. Patrick's Day parades are held each year on a grand scale in cities such as Boston, New York and Chicago, which all boast large Irish-American communities. Seen here is the reviewing stand of the San Francisco St. Patrick's Day Parade. Frank Jordan, the city's popular Irish-American mayor can be seen in the front row, at the right above the green sign. Standing in the back row at the left is Father Michael Healy, the long-time pastor of the city's St. Philip's Parish, a strongly Irish-American community, that also offers masses in Spanish. This is a clear demonstration of the ethnic diversity in this very diverse city. Father Healy is himself an immigrant from County Cork.

St. Patrick's Day Parade 1995

Below: Traditional costumes and traditional dance are part of the vibrant tapestry of any Mexican-American Cinco de Mayo celebration.

Where are They Now?

The United States has been called a nation of immigrants. It is certainly that, and to a larger extent it is a nation of the children and grandchildren of immigrants. When the immigrants arrived in the United States, where did they go, and where are they now?

A great many of them took up residence in the cities where they arrived, with New York City being the most important. New York's magnificent ethnic diversity still bears witness to the immigrants who have arrived there through the years. Other cities of importance were Philadelphia, Boston, Chicago, Milwaukee, Cincinnati, St. Louis and San Francisco, where ethnic neighborhoods are still a vital part of the metropolitan culture.

The initial wave of immigration included the English and Scottish people, who settled throughout New England and south through Virginia to the Carolinas. The Ger-

mans and French arrived in the same areas, particularly in Pennsylvania, where the Germans — or Deutsche — became the "Pennsylvania Dutch."

By the 1840s, as these people were melding into the American culture of "the Melting Pot," the Irish came, escaping the Potato Famine. They arrived in Boston, New York, and Philadelphia and left a mark on those cities that still endures. The Irish made up a large quantity of the laborers who built the subways, but many also joined the police forces and fire departments in the big eastern cities and became one of the dominant ethnicities in the civil service.

The Irish immigrants also went west to work in the mines of Colorado and Montana. In Butte, Montana — where a quarter of the world's copper was mined in the late nineteenth century — the Irish not only worked the mines, but their culture permeated all levels of society in the city that was once the third largest American city west of the Great Plains.

When the Civil War began, recent Irish immigrants joined the Union Army in droves and fought bravely to preserve a nation in which they had lived for but a few months or years. After the war, many of them went to work on the railroads. In fact, the Union Pacific Railroad — the eastern component of the American Transcontinental Railroad — was built largely by "the Irish Tarriers."

Meanwhile, the Central Pacific Railroad — the western component of the American Transcontinental Railroad — was built largely by another important immigrant group, the Chinese. When the Chinese first arrived in the United States as laborers, they were welcomed, but they soon faced an ethnic discrimination that was worse than what had been endured by the Irish in the Eastern United States.

As the ethnic groups arrived in the United States, they sought out places where their countrymen had settled as a way of perpetuating communities of people with a common heritage and culture. The big cities in the East had their Irish and German neighborhoods, just as San Francisco had its Chinatown. But the ethnic groups also spread far and wide.

The Irish went to places such as Butte, and the Germans and central Europeans settled in places such as Cincinnati, Milwaukee, and Sandusky, and there were German communities in in the southwest in Texas, Arizona, and New Mexico. The Chinese were present in the mining camps and cities throughout Colorado and California. The Scandinavians settled in Minnesota and the Dakotas, and everybody seemed to cross paths in Chicago. French-speaking Acadians came from Canada to settle in Louisiana and become "Cajuns."

When the tide of immigration shifted in the late nineteenth century from northern to southern and eastern Europe, the Ital-

ians staked out their own neighborhoods in Boston, New York, Philadelphia, San Francisco, and on the California coast in places such as Santa Cruz. From San Francisco, they went north into the Napa Valley to plant the first vineyards in what would evolve into the most important wine-growing area in the region.

As the Jewish immigration from eastern Europe began, synagogues took their places in neighborhoods adjacent to the Irish and Italian neighborhoods that had grown up around Catholic churches. In San Francisco,

Above: Young Irish-American dancers prepare to compete in a Feis, a traditional Irish dance festival. Dance is an important link between the customs of "the old country" and the American-born, whose grandparents or great grandparents immigrated to the United States.

it was possible to stand on the steps of a Catholic church and see not only a Protestant church, but a synagogue and a roofline of Chinese pagodas.

In the second half of twentieth century, immigration from Asia and Latin America became important. Puerto Ricans immigrated to New York City to take their place alongside the Irish, Germans, and Italians. In the early 1960s, after the Communist takeover of Cuba, Cubans arrived in Florida and now constitute roughly 12 percent of that state's population. In Texas, which has had a sizable Hispanic population since the years when the region was still part of Mexico, a quarter of the state's population is now Hispanic. In New Mexico and Arizona, which, like Texas, share a border with Mexico, the Hispanic populations are 38 and 19 percent respectively.

In California (the most populous state in the United States — with over 30 million people) there are 7. 5 million people of Hispanic origin. These include people with a range of backgrounds, from those who were born in Latin America to those whose families have been in California since statehood in 1850. In the 1990s, California's population was about 30 percent Hispanic and 11 percent Asian, with southern California having a larger percentage of the Hispanic population, and the San Francisco Bay Area having a larger percentage of the Asian population. Indeed, most of the recent Hispanic immigration is concentrated in

Left: The famous Vesuvio Bakery in New York City's Little Italy. During the early nineteenth century, when immigration from Italy exceeded that from any other nation, Little Italy was one of the most important centers of Italian-American culture in North America. Although Italian-American New Yorkers now live throughout the five boroughs, Little Italy still retains many elements of its earlier flavor.

Below: While Little Italy was the center of Italian-American life in New York City, Noe Valley can still be considered to be one of the important Irish-American neighborhoods in San Francisco, and the Dubliner is one of Noe Valley's favorite Irish pubs.

Above: "Ireland's 32" and "Club 25." Irish and Asian businesses side by side are representative of the growing ethnic diversity of American society in the twenty-first century.

brought new faces into the city. A growing Latin American population, which was no longer simply Mexican, flourished in the Mission District. Thus by the 1970s, there were so many different ethnic groups, there was no longer an ethnic majority.

In the San Francisco Bay Area, the Asians now include not only Chinese, but Japanese, Vietnamese, Filipinos, and Koreans. However, in the 1990s, one of the fastest growing immigrant populations in San Francisco was the Irish. As with other new immigrants, first generation Irish immigrants were now walking the same streets as families who had been established for three generations.

So it is, as this new wave of Irish immigration comes at the dawn of the twenty-first century, the nation of immigrants has come full circle, as one of the most ethnically diverse countries on Earth.

Looking Toward the Twenty-first Century

The United States of America enters the twenty-first century as it did the twentieth. It is a nation of immigrants. Over 95 percent of Americans are descended from people that didn't live on this continent in the eighteenth century, and nearly 10 percent of current American citizens were not born in the United States.

In the early years, America was peopled by the English and the Scots. The Irish dominated the years of the 1830s and 1840s, while the Germans led the way from the 1850s through the 1880s, and the Italians were the leading nationality during the first four decades of the twentieth century. Indeed, today, well over half of all Americans list Irish or German among their ethnic roots.

In the latter half of the twentieth century, people from Latin America and the Far East have arrived, bringing with them their unique social customs, ideas, and cultures, which have been added to those contributed by the Swedish Lutherans and Russian Jews, who arrived earlier and still arrive today.

They have all been part of what was called "the melting pot." It is believed that in the first half of the twenty-first century, Hispanics and Asians will account for more than half the growth in the United States population. The biggest expansion of Hispanic and Asian populations will take place in the

three southern California counties: San Diego, Orange, and Los Angeles County, with the latter being about 44 percent Hispanic and 11 percent Asian. In San Francisco, the demographics are roughly the opposite of those in Los Angeles.

San Francisco was long California's foremost melting pot city, just as New York City had been America's foremost melting pot city. By the 1970s, however, San Francisco had become the first major city in the United States to have no minorities. This surprising statistical event occurred because San Francisco had become so diverse that there was no longer a majority. The flight to the suburbs took only a part of the original populations out of what was still a desirable city. Italians who had settled in North Beach in the late nineteenth century, stayed on, but many of those who left, went only as far as the city's Marina District. The Irish of Noe Valley also spread out, but only as far as the city's Sunset District. Chinatown remained Chinatown, but a "new" Chinatown sprang up on Clement Street in the Richmond District, as a new wave of Chinese immigration

Above: In the twenty-first century, Asia is expected to provide a large proportion of the immigrants coming to the United States.

Left: Former immigrants shopping for fireworks for the annual Chinese New Year's celebration.

handful of states that draws the most immigrants, such as California, Texas, New York, Florida, Illinois, and New Jersey — with immigrant communities growing rapidly in such places as Atlanta, Minneapolis, and Washington state.

The Immigration Reform and Control Act and other reforms of the 1980s continued a historical tradition by adapting immigration law and policy to changing United States circumstances. Over the years the sources of immigration shifted. The cultures, languages, and skills of the immigrants changed and became even more diverse. Each of these shifts coincided with growth and change in the United States itself.

During the early years of the nation a policy of open immigration proved beneficial. The United States needed workers and citizens to build the country. By the turn of the century, growing United States industry created a need for immigration legislation. From 1882 until about 1920, mass immigration provided needed workers, while exclusions worked to protect the labor force and United States interests. Beginning in 1891, the Immigration Bureau took charge of regulating that immigration.

Severe restrictions on immigration and limits on the number of immigrants did not occur until the 1920s. The national origins system, lasting from 1921 until the early 1950s, corresponded to a time when United States demand for labor declined. Two world wars in Europe also served to reduce immigration. Through the years of the "Red Scare," the Great Depression, and World War II, Congress expanded the duties of the Immigration and Naturalization Service.

The Service devoted more time to exclusion, deportation, and registration of aliens. The United States' world position changed greatly after World War II, and United States immigration policy slowly adapted to new conditions. Congress passed special legislation to admit refugees and people displaced by the war.

When it was passed, the 1952 Immigration and Nationality Act retained national origins but adjusted policy to include Cold War concerns. The Immigration and Naturalization Service necessarily changed and grew in size. With the wave of European refugees following the war, the Immigration and Naturalization Service began the processing of refugees. Refugee processing remains part of its function in the postwar era.

Social change in the United States in the 1950s and 1960s led to the 1965 amendments, which abandoned the national origins system. Since then, immigrants have been admitted without regard to their nationality within overall numerical limits. Illegal immigration grew during these years as well, and by

the early 1970s the illegal alien problem aroused national concern.

Congress continues to amend and reform Immigration and Naturalization law and policy. In 1986 the Immigration Reform and Control Act dealt with the problem of illegal immigration. The Immigration Act of 1990 revised the system of legal immigration. Future modifications of immigration law and policy can be expected because the questions of immigration change over time.

The final decade of the twentieth century was marked by the largest consistent annual immigration totals in history. The 1,536,483 who entered in 1990 represented an all-time record, but this was exceeded by the 1,877,167 people who entered in 1991. For the remainder of the decade, totals slipped below a million, but dipped below 800,000 only with the 1995 total of 720,461. Demographically, the numbers continued to be high among Latin American and Asian immigrants. There were 1,162,051 Mexicans who entered the United States in 1991-1992, but the numbers declined to 163,743 in 1996. Among other nationalities, European immigration — especially from the former Communist Bloc nations — increased.

Among the western Europeans, Irish immigration was again on the rise, with an increase of nearly 25 percent in the 1993-1994 period alone. In the 1990s, immigration from Romania exceeded all other countries except Mexico, reaching a peak of 64,502 in 1994. Immigration from the Philippines stood at 63,406 in 1993, but dropped to 54,588 in 1996. Arrivals from India peaked at 42,819 in 1996, while immigration from Vietnam peaked at 39,922 in the same year.

Shifting sources of immigration, varying demand for labor in the United States, and the country's humanitarian values all influence the immigration debate. In recent years, as some radical social theorists have favored the paradigm of isolating vari-

ous ethnic groups, most immigrants have continued to contribute their unique perspectives to the melting pot that has made the American nationality unique in all the world. In the twenty-first century, immigration will continue to be an important part of American history and a defining factor in the American national identity.

Above: Soccer balls and the Virgin of Guadalupe are symbolic of the cultural elements that Latin-American culture has brought to the American national identity.

Right: The notion of ethnic diversity in the United States at the beginning of the twenty-first century — as represented by its many immigrant groups — is symbolized by this image of an American street scene. Gaspare's Pizza and Italian Dinners has obviously been in place since the middle of the twentieth century, and it has been joined by the Moscow & Tblisi Russian Bakery (although Tblisi is in Georgia). Next door, Henry's offers "American Food" in Chinese and English lettering. The Qi Gong Seafood Restaurant, in turn, offers Hakka cuisine next door to Kojimoto, a Japanese-American printing firm.

While by no means a "typical" business street in the United States, this image certainly sums up the essence of the American melting pot of nationalities.

Included in this glossary are terms used in this book as well as terms used officially by such United States agencies as the Bureau of Immigration and Naturalization.

Acquired Citizenship: Citizenship conferred at birth for children born abroad to a citizen parent(s).

Adjustment to Immigrant Status: Procedure allowing certain aliens already in the United States to apply for immigrant status. An alien admitted to the United States in a nonimmigrant or other category may have his or her status changed to that of lawful permanent resident if he or she is eligible to receive an immigrant visa as a permanent resident and an immigrant visa is immediately available. In such cases, the alien is counted as an immigrant as of the date of adjustment even though the alien may have been in the United States for an extended period of time.

Admission: The lawful entry of an alien or a citizen into the United States through a port of entry.

Alien: Any person not a citizen or a national of the United States.

Alien Address Report Program: A now-defunct annual registration program for aliens. Until Public Law 97-116 (Act of December 29, 1981) eliminated the stipulation, all aliens in the United States were required to register with the Immigration and Naturalization Service each January. Nationality and state of residence data were compiled annually on the alien population reporting under the program. The last year for which data is available is 1980.

Apprehension: The arrest of a deportable alien by the Immigration and Naturalization Service. Each apprehension of the same alien in a fiscal year is counted separately.

Asylee (Asylum): An alien physically present in the United States or at a port of entry may request asylum in the United States. The definition of an asylee is essentially the same as a refugee. The only difference is the location of the alien upon application; the asylee is in the United States or at a port of entry and the refugee is overseas. According to the Refugee Act of 1980, current immigration status, whether legal or illegal is not relevant to an individual's asylum claim. Asylees are eligible to adjust to lawful permanent resident status after one year of continuous presence in the United States. While these immigrants are exempt from the numerical limitations of the INA, the act does stipulate how many asylees can adjust per fiscal year.

Beneficiary: An alien who receives immigration benefits from petitions filed with the Immigration and Naturalization Service. A beneficiary generally derives privilege or status as a result of his or her relationship (including that of employer-employee) to a United States citizen or lawful permanent resident.

Border Crosser: An alien or citizen resident of the United States reentering the country across land borders after an absence of less than six months in Canada or Mexico, or a nonresident alien entering the United States across the Canadian border for stays of no more than six months or across the Mexican border for stays of no more than 72 hours, or a United States citizen residing in Canada or Mexico who enters the United States frequently for business or pleasure.

Border Patrol Sector: Any one of 21 geographic areas into which the United States is divided for the Immigration and Naturalization Service's Border Patrol activities. Of the 21 sectors, all but one are located along the northern and southern borders of the United States.

Certificate of Citizenship: Identity document proving United States citizenship. Certificates of citizenship are issued to derivative citizens and to persons who acquired United States citizenship (see definitions for acquired and derivative citizenship).

Citizen (United States): A person who is born in the United States or who became a naturalized citizen of the United States.

Consul/Consular Officer: Any consular, diplomatic, or other officer of the United States who issues immigrant and nonimmigrant visas according to regulations prescribed by the Immigration and Nationality Act.

Country of Former Allegiance: The previous country of citizenship of a naturalized United States citizen or of a person who derived United States citizenship.

Country of Last Residence: The country in which an alien habitually resided prior to entering another.

Crewman: A foreign national serving in any capacity on board a vessel or aircraft.

Cuban/Haitian Entrant Status: Status accorded to (1) Cubans who entered the United States between April 15, 1980, and October 20, 1980 from Mariel Harbor and (2) Haitians who entered the country illegally before January 1, 1981. Cubans and Haitians meeting these criteria who have lived in the United States since before January 1, 1982, may adjust to permanent resident status under a provision of the Immigration Reform and Control Act.

Declaration of Intention: Before 1952, a form filed by a lawful permanent resident as the first step toward naturalization. After two years residence as an immigrant, the alien could file a declaration of intention. Now it is usually filed only to obtain a professional license.

Deportable Alien: An alien in the United States subject to any of the 19 grounds of deportation specified in the Immigration and Nationality Act. This includes any alien illegally in the United States, regardless of whether the alien entered the country illegally or entered legally but subsequently violated the terms of his or her visa.

Deportation: The formal removal of an alien from the United States when the presence of that alien is deemed inconsistent with the public welfare. Deportation is ordered by an immigration judge without any punishment being imposed or contemplated.

Derivative Citizenship: Citizenship conveyed to children through the naturalization of parents or, under certain circumstances, to spouses of citizens at marriage.

Dual Citizenship or Dual Nationality: A person who is a citizen of more than one nation or state. This is common for people born in one nation or state to parents who are citizens of another nation or state. The United States does not recognize dual citizenship.

Emigrant: A person who leaves one country to live in another country.

Employer Sanctions: In the United States, under the prohibition of the unlawful employment of illegal aliens, sanction policy provides for penalties and fines against employers who hire, recruit, or refer aliens to employment for a fee. Employers are required to verify the eligibility of all workers they hire. Sanctions also punish employers who continue to employ unauthorized aliens. The purpose of sanctions is to remove the incentive for illegal immigration by eliminating the job pool for unauthorized workers.

Excludable Aliens: Those aliens who may be denied admission into this country on grounds specified in the Immigration and Nationality Act.

Exclusion: The formal denial of an alien's entry into the United States. The exclusion of the alien is made by an immigration judge after an exclusion hearing.

Exempt from Numerical Limitations: Those aliens accorded lawful permanent residence who are exempt from the provisions of the preference system set forth in immigration law. Exempt categories include immediate relatives of United States citizens, refugees, special immigrants, and certain other immigrants.

Expatriation: The loss of citizenship as a result of a formal transference of loyalties to another country.

Fiscal Year: The 12-month period beginning October 1 and running through September 30. Prior to fiscal 1977, the fiscal year ran from July 1 through June 30.

Foreign State of Chargeability: The independent country to which an immigrant entering under the preference system is accredited. Independent countries cannot exceed 20,000 immigrants in a fiscal year. Dependencies of independent countries cannot exceed 600 of the 20,000 limit. Chargeability is usually determined by country of birth. Exceptions are made to prevent the separation of family members when the limitation for the country of birth has been met.

Geographic Area of Chargeability: Any one of five regions — Africa, East Asia, Latin America and the Caribbean, the Near East, and South Asia, and the former Soviet Union and eastern Europe — into which the world is divided for the initial admission of refugees to the United States. Annual consultations between the executive branch and the Congress determine the number of refugees that can be admitted to the United States from each area.

Hemispheric Ceilings: Statutory limits on immigration to the United States in effect from 1968 to October 1978. Mandated by the Immigration and Nationality Act Amendments of 1965, the ceiling on immigration from the Eastern Hemisphere was set at 170,000, with a per-country limit of 20,000. Immigration from the Western Hemisphere was held to 120,000, without a per-country limit until January 1, 1977. The Western Hemisphere was then subject to a 20,000 per-country limit.

ICM: Intergovernmental Committee on Migration (United States government acronym).

IMDAC: Immigrant Data Capture System (United States government acronym).

INA: Immigration and Nationality Act (United States government acronym).

INS: Immigration and Naturalization Service (United States government acronym).

IRCA: Immigration Reform and Control Act of 1986 (United States government acronym).

Illegal Alien: (1) A foreign national who entered the United States, without inspection or with fraudulent documentation. (2) A foreign national who, after entering legally as a nonimmigrant, violated status and remained in the United States without authority.

Immediate Relatives: Certain immigrants who, because of their close relationship to United States citizens, are exempt from the numerical limitations imposed on immigration to the United States.

Immediate relatives are: spouses of citizens, children (under 21 years of age) of citizens, parents of citizens 21 years of age or older, and orphans adopted by United States citizens who are at least 21 years of age.

Immigrant: A citizen of one country admitted to another country as a lawful permanent resident. The United States Immigration and Naturalization Service defines immigrants as those persons lawfully accorded the privilege of residing permanently in the United States. They may be issued immigrant visas by the Department of State overseas or adjusted to permanent resident status by the Immigration and Naturalization Service in the United States.

Immigrant Visa: A document issued by a United States Consul abroad. It authorizes an alien to apply for admission as an immigrant to the United States.

Immigration and Nationality Act: One of a series of laws enacted by the United States government to regulate immigration into the United States. **Immigration and Naturalization Service (INS):** A part of the United States Justice Department, the Immigration and Naturalization Service is the United States government agency charged with enforcing immigration law, as well as with maintaining statistics about and providing services for immigrants.

International Migration: A change of residence across national boundaries.

Inspection: The examination by an immigration officer of a person applying for admission to the United States. The officer verifies the person's identity, nationality, and

whether he/she is legally entitled to enter.

Intern (Internee): A person of enemy nationality restricted or confined to a limited territory, especially during wartime. Such confinement of enemy aliens is governed by the Geneva Convention.

Internment: To restrict or confine a person of enemy nationality to a limited territory, especially during wartime. Such confinement of enemy aliens is governed by the Geneva Convention.

Labor Certification: Certification by the Secretary of Labor that the entry of certain aliens for work purposes will not harm the United States labor market. It certifies:
1) There are not enough United States workers ready, willing and able to do that particular labor.
2) That the alien's employment in the United States will not adversely affect the wages and working conditions of people similarly employed in the United States. Certain applications for permanent residence require labor certification, as do certain nonimmigrant categories.

Legalized Alien: Certain illegal aliens are eligible to apply for temporary resident status under the legalization provision of the Immigration Reform and Control Act of 1986. To be eligible, aliens must have been in the United States in an unlawful status since January 1, 1982, not be excludable, and have entered the United States either illegally or as temporary visitors before January 1, 1982. Legalization has two stages—temporary and then permanent residency.

MIRAC: Master Index Remote Access Capability System (United States government acronym).
Moral Turpitude, Crime involving: An act that is basically wrong, evil, depraved, or offensive to society.

NCHS: National Center for Health Statistics (United States government acronym).

NIDC: Nonimmigrant Document Control System (United States government acronym).

NIIS: Nonimmigrant Information System (United States government acronym).

Nationality: The country of a person's citizenship. For nonimmigrants, nationality refers to the alien's claimed country of citizenship.

Naturalization: The conferring, by any means, of citizenship upon a person after birth.

Naturalization Court: Any court authorized to award United States citizenship. Jurisdiction for naturalization has been conferred upon the following courts:
United States District Courts in all states, the District of Columbia, and Puerto Rico; the District Courts of Guam and the Virgin Islands; and state courts. Generally naturalization courts are authorized to award citizenship only to those persons who reside within their territorial jurisdiction.

Naturalization Petition: The form used by a lawful permanent resident to apply for United States citizenship. The petition is filed with a naturalization court through the Immigration and Naturalization Service. (Various other petitions are also filed for other immigrant benefits).

Naturalization Provisions (General): The basic requirements for naturalization that every applicant must meet, unless a member of a special class. General provisions require an applicant to be at least 18 years of age, a lawful permanent resident with five years of continuous residence in the United States, and to have been physically

Number and Nationality of Immigrants Arrived in the United States during the Ten Fiscal Years (July 1st to June 30th,) 1882 to 1891.

NATIONALITY.		1882	1883	1884	1885	1886	1887	1888	1889	1890	1891
All Countries Not Specified		103,289	74,729	67,310	45,567	6,720	11,164	12,269	11,218	9,357	8,666
Asia {	Rest of Asia	50	82	231	176	277	605	817	1,607	2,732	4,842
	China	39,579	8,031	279	22	40	10	26	118	1,716	2,836
	(total)	39,629	8,113	510	198	317	615	843	1,725	4,448	7,678
Europe Not Specified		260	236	425	1,113	774	2,564	2,175	1,303	1,247	2,327
Spain and Portugal {	Spain	378	262	300	350	344	436	626	626	813	905
	Portugal	42	176	701	440	238	110	23	57	158	918
	(total)	420	438	1,001	790	582	646	649	683	971	1,823
Belgium and France {	Belgium	1,431	1,450	1,576	1,653	1,300	2,553		2,562	2,671	3,037
	France	6,004	4,821	3,608	3,495	3,318	5,034	6,464	5,918	6,595	6,770
	(total)	7,435	6,271	5,184	5,148	4,618	7,587	9,669	8,480	9,266	9,807
Netherlands		9,517	5,249	4,198	2,689	2,314	4,506	5,845	6,460	4,326	5,206
Denmark		11,618	10,319	9,202	6,100	6,225	8,524	8,962	8,699	9,366	10,659
Switzerland		10,844	12,751	9,386	5,895	4,805	5,214	7,737	7,070	6,993	6,811
Poland		4,672	2,011	4,536	3,085	3,939	6,128	5,826	4,922	11,073	27,497
Austria-Hungary {	Bohemia	6,602	5,462	8,239	6,352	4,314	4,579	4,127	3,085	4,505	11,758
	Hungary	8,929	11,240	14,798	9,383	12,420	15,256	15,900	10,967	22,062	28,366
	Rest (except) Poland	13,619	10,923	13,534	11,574	11,946	20,430	26,894	20,122	29,632	30,918
	(total)	29,150	27,635	36,571	27,309	28,680	40,265	46,811	34,174	56,199	71,042
Russia (except Poland)		16,918	10,909	12,689	17,158	17,800	30,766	33,487	33,916	35,983	47,426
Norway and Sweden {	Norway	29,101	23,398	16,974	12,356	12,759	16,269	18,264	13,390	11,370	12,568
	Sweden	64,607	38,277	26,552	22,248	27,751	42,836	54,698	35,415	29,632	36,880
	(total)	93,708	61,676	43,626	34,604	40,510	59,105	72,962	48,806	41,002	49,448
Italy		32,059	31,792	16,510	13,642	21,315	47,622	51,558	26,307	52,003	76,065
Great Britain and Ireland {	Rest	1,670	1,607	980	1,159	1,051	1,937	1,692	1,206	679	467
	Scotland	18,937	11,859	9,060	9,226	12,126	18,699	24,457	18,296	12,641	12,557
	Ireland	76,432	81,486	63,344	51,795	49,619	68,370	73,513	65,557	53,024	55,706
	England	82,394	63,740	55,918	47,332	49,767	72,855	82,574	68,503	57,020	53,600
	(total)	179,433	163,092	129,302	109,612	112,663	161,761	182,226	153,562	122,764	112,330
Germany		250,630	194,786	179,676	124,443	84,403	106,865	109,717	99,538	92,427	113,554
Total		788,992	603,322	518,592	395,346	334,203	490,109	546,889	444,427	455,302	560,319

NOTE: Immigrants from the British North American Possessions and Mexico are not included since July 1st, 1885.

Number of Immigrants, by Periods, Arrived in the United States during the 103 Years, 1789 to 1891.

SCALE : ⅔ of Scale for Main Diagram.

1789–1819	250,000 (estimated)
1820–1831	170,968
1832–1841	643,645
1842–1851	1,972,180
1852–1861	2,262,459
1862–1871	2,530,222
1872–1881	3,162,272
1882–1891	5,137,501

present in the country for half that period.

New Arrival: A lawful permanent resident alien who enters the United States at a port of entry. The alien is generally required to present an immigrant visa issued outside the United States by a consular officer of the Department of State.

Three classes of immigrants, however, need not have an immigrant visa to enter the United States — children born abroad to lawful permanent resident aliens, children born subsequent to the issuance of an immigrant visa to accompanying parents, and American Indians born in Canada.

Nonimmigrant: An alien who seeks temporary entry to the United States for a specific purpose. The alien must have a permanent residence abroad and qualify for nonimmigrant classification.

The United States Immigration and Naturalization Service defines a nonimmigrant as one without immigrant status. Nonimmigrants include: foreign government officials, officials and employees of international organizations, visitors for business and pleasure, crewmen, students, trainees, and temporary workers of distinguished merit and ability or who perform services unavailable in the United States. Refugees are also considered nonimmigrants when initially admitted.

ORR: Office of Refugee Resettlement (United States government acronym).

Occupation: For an alien entering the United States or adjusting without a labor certification, occupation refers to the employment held in the country of last or legal residence or the United States. For an alien with a labor certification, occupation is the employment for which certification has been issued. Labor certification would be issued to immigrants in the third, sixth, and nonpreference categories, or to nonim-

migrant temporary workers performing services unavailable in the United States.

Parole: The temporary admission of an otherwise inadmissible alien under emergency (humanitarian) conditions, or when that alien's entry is determined to be in the public interest. Parole is not a formal admission to the United States. It confers temporary admission status only, requiring parolees to leave when the conditions supporting their parole cease to exist.

Parolee: An alien allowed to enter the United States under emergency conditions, or when that alien's entry is determined to be in the public interest.

Permanent Resident Alien: A person entering this country with an immigrant visa, or adjusting to this status after having entered as a nonimmigrant or as a refugee or asylee. Permanent resident status entitles an immigrant to live and work in the United States.

Port of Entry: Any location in the United States or its territories which is designated as a point of entry for aliens and United States citizens. All district control offices are also considered ports since they become locations of entry for aliens adjusting to immigrant status.

Preference System: The six categories among which a specified number of immigrant visas are distributed each year.

Principal Alien: The alien from whom another alien derives a privilege or status under immigration law or regulation.

Private Bill: Special legislation introduced in Congress to benefit an individual alien.

RPG: Refugee Policy Group (United States government acronym).

Refugee: Any person who is outside his or her country of nationality and is unable or unwilling to return to that country because of persecution or a well founded fear of persecution. Persecution or the fear of it may be based on the alien's race, religion, nationality, membership in a particular social group, or political opinion. People with no nationality must be outside their country of last habitual residence to qualify as a refugee. See also Asylee.

Refugee Approvals: The number of refugees approved for admission to the United States during a fiscal year. Refugee approvals are made by Immigration and Naturalization Service officers in overseas offices.

Registry Date: The date from which an illegal alien has resided illegally and continuously in the United States.

Repatriation: To restore or return to the country of birth or citizenship.

Required Departure: The directed departure of an alien from the United States without an order of deportation. The departure may be voluntary or involuntary on the part of the alien, and may or may not have been preceded by a hearing before an immigration judge.

Special Immigrants: Certain categories of immigrants exempt from numerical limitations on visa issuance—persons who lost citizenship by marriage; persons who lost citizenship by serving in foreign armed forces; ministers of religion, their spouses and children; certain employees or former employees of the United States government abroad, their spouses and children; and Panama Canal Act immigrants.

Special Naturalization Provisions: Under United States law, these are provisions covering special classes of persons who may be naturalized, even though they do not meet all the general requirements for naturalization. Such special provisions allow (1) wives or husbands of United States citizens to be naturalized in three years instead of the prescribed five years (2) a surviving spouse of a United States citizen who served in the armed forces to file in any naturalization court instead of where he or she resides, (3) children of United States citizen parents to be naturalized without meeting the literacy or government-knowledge requirements or taking the oath, if too young to understand its meaning.

Other classes of persons who may qualify for special consideration are former United States citizens, servicemen, seamen, and employees of organizations promoting United States interests abroad.

Stateless: The condition of a person having no nationality.

Steerage: A term applied to the inexpensive — and often windowless — passenger accommodations in the lower part of a ship near the rudder, where the ship is steered. Many poor immigrants traveled to the United States in steerage.

Subject to Numerical Limitations: A condition imposed on all immigration to the United States, except for the immediate relatives of United States citizens and certain special immigrants. The number of aliens accorded lawful permanent residence under the provisions of the preference system must not exceed 270,000 in any fiscal year. The preference system provides for the admission of relatives of

citizens (other than immediate relatives), immediate relatives of lawful permanent resident aliens, and aliens in specified occupations, as well as other immigrants.

Suspension of Deportation: A discretionary benefit adjusting an alien's status from that of deportable alien to one of lawfully admitted for permanent residence. Application for suspension of deportation is made during a deportation hearing before an immigration judge. The alien must show continuous United States residence for at least seven years and that extreme hardship would result from deportation.

Temporary Resident: An alien who has been adjusted to temporary resident status under the provisions of the Immigration Reform and Control Act

of 1986 (IRCA). Temporary resident status is of limited duration. Temporary residents must adjust to permanent resident status.

Temporary Worker: Aliens temporarily admitted to the United States to perform specific work. Examples include: services of an exceptional nature, temporary labor where unemployed United States workers cannot be found, or for professional training.

Undocumented Alien: An alien without proper documents showing legal entry into the United States. Although an undocumented alien could be someone who accidentally misplaced their passport, this term is generally used to mean illegal alien.

Violation of Status: Violation of the conditions under which an alien was admitted to the United States. Example: a nonimmigrant alien admitted as a student to attend school violates nonimmigrant status if he or she fails to attend school, or takes unauthorized employment.

Voluntary Departure: Allowing an alien who is in violation of the immigration laws to depart the United States voluntarily rather than being formally deported. Voluntary departure may also be accorded to a person granted asylum status who is not in violation of immigration laws.

Left: The Japanese-American community in San Francisco.

Immigration to the United States by Nation of Origin from 1820 Through the End of the Twentieth Century

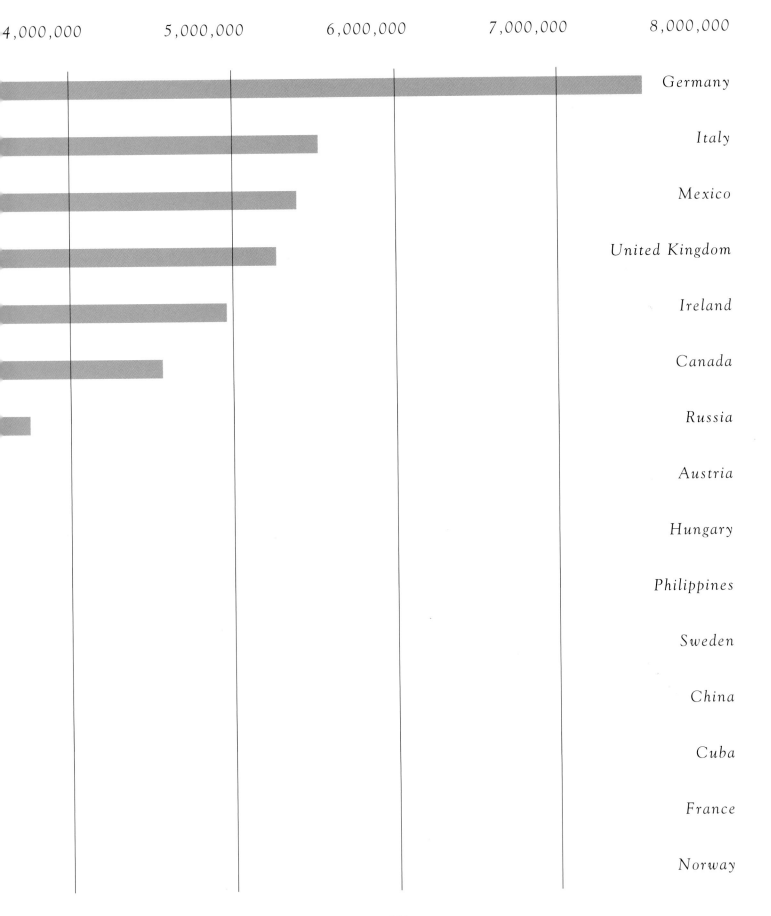

Immigration to the United States by Nation of Origin
from 1820 Through the End of the Twentieth Century

4,000,000   5,000,000   6,000,000   7,000,000   8,000,000

Germany

Italy

Mexico

United Kingdom

Ireland

Canada

Russia

Austria

Hungary

Philippines

Sweden

China

Cuba

France

Norway